Great Composers

Other Books in the History Makers Series:

History MAKERS

Great Composers

By Stuart A. Kallen

Lucent Books
P.O. Box 289011, San Diego, CA 92198-9011

On Cover: *Wolfgang Amadeus Mozart (background), Ludwig van Beethoven (top right), George and Ira Gershwin (bottom right), Johann Sebastian Bach (bottom left).*

Library of Congress Cataloging-in-Publication Data

Kallen, Stuart A., 1955–
    Great composers / by Stuart A. Kallen.
        p.   cm. — (History makers)
    Includes bibliographical references and index.
    Summary: Discusses the lives and works of such well-known composers as Bach, Mozart, Beethoven, Tchaikovsky, Puccini, Gershwin, and Weber.
    ISBN 1-56006-669-5 (lib. bdg. : alk. paper)
    1. Composers—Biography—Juvenile literature [1. Composers.] I. Title. II. Series.

ML3929 .K35 2000
780'.92'2—dc21
[B]
                                                                99-058597

19.95

CONTENTS

The literary form most often referred to as "multiple biography" was perfected in the first century A.D. by Plutarch, a perceptive and talented moralist and historian who hailed from the small town of Chaeronea in central Greece. His most famous work, *Parallel Lives*, consists of a long series of biographies of noteworthy ancient Greek and Roman statesmen and military leaders. Frequently, Plutarch compares a famous Greek to a famous Roman, pointing out similarities in personality and achievements. These expertly constructed and very readable tracts provided later historians and others, including playwrights like Shakespeare, with priceless information about prominent ancient personages and also inspired new generations of writers to tackle the multiple biography genre.

The Lucent History Makers series proudly carries on the venerable tradition handed down from Plutarch. Each volume in the series consists of a set of five to eight biographies of important and influential historical figures who were linked together by a common factor. In *Rulers of Ancient Rome*, for example, all the figures were generals, consuls, or emperors of either the Roman Republic or Empire; while the subjects of *Fighters Against American Slavery*, though they lived in different places and times, all shared the same goal, namely the eradication of human servitude. Mindful that politicians and military leaders are not (and never have been) the only people who shape the course of history, the editors of the series have also included representatives from a wide range of endeavors, including scientists, artists, writers, philosophers, religious leaders, and sports figures.

Each book is intended to give a range of figures—some well known, others less known; some who made a great impact on history, others who made only a small impact. For instance, by making Columbus's initial voyage possible, Spain's Queen Isabella I, featured in *Women Leaders of Nations*, helped to open up the New World to exploration and exploitation by the European powers. Unarguably, therefore, she made a major contribution to a series of events that had momentous consequences for the entire world. By contrast, Catherine II, the eighteenth-century Russian queen, and Golda Meir, the modern Israeli prime minister, did not play roles of global impact; however, their policies and actions significantly influenced the historical development of both their own countries and their regional neighbors. Regardless of their relative importance in the greater historical scheme, all of the figures chronicled in the History Makers series made contributions to posterity; and their public achievements, as well as what is known about their private lives, are presented and evaluated in light of the most recent scholarship.

In addition, each volume in the series is documented and substantiated by a wide array of primary and secondary source quotations. The primary source quotes enliven the text by presenting eyewitness views of the times and culture in which each history maker lived; while the secondary source quotes, taken from the works of respected modern scholars, offer expert elaboration and/ or critical commentary. Each quote is footnoted, demonstrating to the reader exactly where biographers find their information. The footnotes also provide the reader with the means of conducting additional research. Finally, to further guide and illuminate readers, each volume in the series features photographs, two bibliographies, and a comprehensive index.

The History Makers series provides both students engaged in research and more casual readers with informative, enlightening, and entertaining overviews of individuals from a variety of circumstances, professions, and backgrounds. No doubt all of them, whether loved or hated, benevolent or cruel, constructive or destructive, will remain endlessly fascinating to each new generation seeking to identify the forces that shaped their world.

Music from the Heart to the Heart

Prior to the twentieth century, when jazz, rhythm-and-blues, country-and-western, rock-and-roll, and pop music entered the scene, almost all music was what we today call "classical music." From the 1700s to the 1900s, classical music composed for orchestras or for instruments such as violins, pianos, and even guitars was played everywhere from concert halls to restaurants to the living rooms of ordinary people.

American composer George Gershwin.

Before there were rock concerts there were musical events such as public performances of symphonies and operas where people dressed up, partied with their friends, and breathlessly ogled at their favorite musical stars. And the great composers in this book, from Ludwig van Beethoven to George Gershwin, were the musical idols of their day. People followed their careers, wrote about them in newspapers, gossiped about their private lives, and often made them rich and famous.

Many of the world's greatest composers, such as Johann Bach, Wolfgang Mozart, Beethoven, Giacomo Puccini, and Andrew Lloyd Webber came from musical families. They were exposed to music as babies, focused their talents at a very early age, and were able to find work because of family connections. Others, such as Pyotr Tchaikovsky and Gershwin, were simply tuned into melody and excelled because of a passionate love of music.

Like the pop idols of today, the great composers were only human. They had frailties, faults, weaknesses, and health problems just like any other person. While not all great composers led tragic lives, many were outsiders to society: Mozart was a flamboyant egotist who defied cultural convention, Beethoven was isolated because of his deafness, and Tchaikovsky because of his homosexuality. Nevertheless, they rose above the setbacks and the tough competition from other musicians to define the standards of greatness that we still use today.

In most cases this lack of conformity pitted the talents of the composers against politicians, religious leaders, and rulers of the day. The groundbreaking music of Beethoven's Third Symphony was called "decadent" by critics who—more than 150 years prior to rock critics—feared that its rhythms would lead to lewd behavior. Puccini's opera *Madama Butterfly* was met with jeers, hissing, and mocking laughter. The religious content of Lloyd Webber's rock opera *Jesus Christ Superstar* sparked widespread protest from the United States to New Zealand.

While the critics and commentators have faded into history, unknown and unremembered, those who wrote the music of their souls are, in most cases, more popular today than they were at the time of their deaths. The sounds of the great composers are heard the world over today from people playing from sheet music and CDs and listening to MP3s on dozens of Internet websites. Movies such as

Wolfgang Amadeus Mozart plays his opera Don Giovanni *for the first time in Vienna.*

Amadeus about Mozart and *Immortal Beloved* about Beethoven were box-office hits; meanwhile, the operas of Puccini and the musicals of Lloyd Webber continue to break attendance records on Broadway and beyond.

Famous composers such as Mozart and Beethoven were not alone in shaping what we call classical music today. No single book can detail the lives of all those who were important—Antonio Vivaldi, Johannes Brahms, Claude Debussy, Igor Stravinsky, Gustav Mahler, and so many, many more. These men lived in different centuries and spoke many languages, including Italian, German, French, and Russian. But their music has transcended the barriers of time and language.

Music speaks its own language, which may be understood by a baby or even by a hearing-impaired musician like Beethoven. It has a way of bringing people together with its harmony and rhythm and of helping people escape from their daily problems, if even for a few moments. For that reason, the great composers, many of whom sacrificed personal happiness for their art, are remembered as heroes. Perhaps Beethoven stated it most eloquently when he wrote the dedication atop his astounding Ninth Symphony: In spite of his personal suffering, the music was: "From the heart—may it go to the heart."[1]

CHAPTER 1

Johann Sebastian Bach

By the time Johann Sebastian was born in the central German state of Thuringia, the Bach family had produced several generations of well-known, skilled musicians. In fact, the name *Bach* had come to be used interchangeably with the word *musician* in the region. The reason for this is explained in *The Bach Reader*, edited by Hans T. David and Arthur Mendel:

> Up to and including [Johann Sebastian] Bach's time, most German musicians earned their living by entering the regular service of a noble or princely patron as court or chamber musician; of a town council as town piper; or of a municipal or ecclesiastical authority as church organist, music director, or cantor—the latter function including the teaching of music in a school. Most [members of the Bach family] were town or church musicians, and so many of them were members of certain . . . Thuringian musical "companies" that . . . the town musicians were called [in German] *"die Baache"* long after the last Bach had ceased to serve in such a capacity.[2]

The Bach family lived in the town of Eisenach in a large home near the town center. Johann Sebastian was born on March 21, 1685, the eighth child of Johann Ambrosius and Elizabeth Bach. The baby's father was an accomplished musician who performed ceremonial music at the town hall and later took a job as a court trumpeter for the duke of Eisenach.

As would be expected in a musical family such as the Bachs, all of Johann Ambrosius's children received comprehensive musical educations. Johann Sebastian was taught at an early age by his father to play the violin and the harpsichord, a keyboard instrument that preceded the piano. As a young man, Johann Sebastian would sit in the organ loft next to his uncle Johann Christoph Bach, the organist at Eisenach's St. George's Church, and observe him writing and playing music. Before long, the young Johann was a remarkably accomplished player of the violin and keyboards.

When he was eight years old, Johann Sebastian attended the Latin Grammar School. The young man learned reading, writing, Latin grammar, and a great deal of scripture in both Latin and German. When the boys in school formed a choir at St. George's Church, Johann Sebastian joined, and his rich soprano could soon be heard at regular services and in nearby village churches.

The Young Prodigy

Sadly, the pleasant musical life of Johann Sebastian was soon interrupted by tragedy. First, a sister died, then a brother. Then, when he was nine years old, his mother died. His father died barely nine months later. Left as an orphan without a home, Johann Sebastian and one of his brothers, Johann Jakob, were taken into the home of their eldest brother, Johann Christoph, who had recently married and moved to the small town of Ohrdruf, located thirty miles southeast of Eisenach. Johann Christoph had been a pupil of the famous composer Pachelbel, and at the time the eldest Bach was a well-known organist at St. Michaeliskirche (St. Michael's Church).

Johann Christoph gave his young brother organ lessons and taught him to hand-copy music by German organ composers in order to learn composition. In the spring of 1700, Johann Sebastian set out on foot for the Michaelis monastery, which was situ-

The house where Johann Sebastian Bach was born on March 21, 1685, in Eisenach, Germany.

ated in Lüneburg some 180 miles away. The young man had been hired as a choir boy at the well-to-do monastery, which was known to charitably provide lodging for poor boys with musical talent.

Because of his uncommonly beautiful voice, Johann Sebastian was immediately appointed to the elite "Mattins Choir," which participated in elaborate choral and orchestral performances. His position also entitled him to study in the school's fine musical library, which included some of the best examples of German church music. As Bach grew older, he lost his high soprano voice. But he stayed on as a violinist and accompanied the choir on the harpsichord during rehearsals.

A Young Organist at New Church

At the age of eighteen, Bach decided to return to his native Thuringia, where an organ was under construction at a new church in Arnstadt. Since his family had been professionally active in the town for generations, he felt that he might be appointed to the post of church organist. In 1703 the Arnstadt Town Council invited Bach to try out for the now-finished organ in "New Church." People were so impressed with his playing that he was immediately appointed as the new organist and was offered a good salary. As part of his job, Bach was expected to play on all Sundays, feast days, and other times of public worship. In addition to maintaining the church organ, the town fathers wrote in a contract that Bach was to be "God-fearing, temperate, well-disposed to all folk, eschewing ill company, and in all ways show yourself an honourable servant and organist before God and your worshipful masters."[3]

Bach was enthusiastic about his new job and began to compose dozens of pieces of music. For his first Easter at New Church, he wrote a cantata—a type of composition featuring recited words, vocal choruses, and solos, with instrumental accompaniment. For this cantata, Bach assembled an orchestra of strings, three trumpets, and drums to support his choir. The people attending services at New Church were amazed by the brilliant performance. Bach, however, did not let the adoration go to his head. He wrote this piece—and all of his music—as a tribute to God. For, as Bach told his musical students in a statement that can be found in *The Bach Reader,* "The aim and final reason . . . of all music . . . should be none else but the Glory of God and the recreation of the mind. Where this is not observed, there will be no real music but only a devilish hubbub."[4]

In October 1705, when the great organist Dietrich Buxtehude played in the northern city of Lübeck, Bach received a one-month leave of absence to hear Buxtehude play. The composer walked 199 miles to Lübeck, where he met the organist. The young man was so fascinated by Buxtehude's brilliant technique that he remained in Lübeck to study with him until the following February, returning to Arnstadt three months later than expected.

Bach's experience had given him exciting new musical ideas that he played for the surprised and bewildered Arnstadt congregation.

Bach served as the church organist in Arnstadt from 1703 to 1706.

Bach was called before the church council and was reprimanded, first for his four-month absence and then for his new style of playing. The words of the council were recorded in Charles Sanford Terry's *Johann Sebastian Bach:*

> Complaints have been made . . . that you now accompany the hymns with surprising variations and irrelevant ornaments, which obliterate the melody and confuse the congregation. If you desire to introduce a theme against the melody, you must go on with it and not immediately fly off to another. And under no circumstances must you introduce a *tonus contrarius* [tone conflicting with the melody].[5]

Although the men on the church council were upset, they knew that their talented young organist was irreplaceable, so they treated him with leniency. Other conflicts soon arose with the council, however, over Bach's unwillingness to train the undisciplined boys' choir. Before long the organist was looking for work elsewhere.

At the end of 1706, Bach was hired as a church organist by the town of Mühlhausen. His annual salary, according to city documents was, "85 gulden in money . . . 54 bushels of grain, [and] 2 cords of wood, 1 beech and 1 oak or aspen."[6]

"His Feet Had Wings"

As Bach assumed his position as organist for the church in Mühlhausen, his maternal uncle Tobias Lämmerhirt died, leaving him an inheritance. This enabled Bach to marry his cousin from Arnstadt, Maria Barbara Bach, on October 17, 1707. Bach's new wife came from one of the musical branches of the Bach family—her father was an organist in the town of Gehren. Together the couple would have seven children.

At Mühlhausen, Bach began training the choir and a newly created orchestra to play his music. He was also assigned the task of restoring the organ he was assigned to play, for by this time he was also an expert on the mechanical workings of the complicated instrument. And in 1708, he wrote a cantata called "Gott ist mein König" ("God Is My King") to celebrate the inauguration of the town council. Although Bach wrote more than three hundred cantatas, this was the only one ever published in his lifetime.

Before long, however, a religious controversy arose in Mühlhausen between the Orthodox Lutherans, who were lovers of music, and the Pietists, who were very conservative and did not believe dramatic music should be played in church. Not wishing to be involved in this controversy, Bach turned in a letter of resignation on June 25, 1708, writing, "I have not been allowed to do my work without opposition, and there does not seem to be the least appearance that it will abate."[7]

Bach was now off to the small town of Weimar, where the duke of Sachsen-Weimar offered him a position among his court chamber musicians. The court orchestra consisted of twenty-two musicians: a compact string ensemble, a bassoon player, six trumpeters, and a timpani, or kettledrum, player. Bach mainly played violin, but he also wrote and arranged music and filled in on harpsichord. As was the custom in courts at that time, the musicians had to spend time employed in various household duties, and Bach, like the other musicians, was given a servant's uniform to wear.

At Weimar, Bach had more freedom to compose, and many of his greatest organ works were written during this period. He was becoming known throughout the entire country as one of the greatest German organists, and students came from all over to learn from the master. Many towns and villages requested that Bach test or repair their organs, and his tests were very thorough and critical. When Bach finished his inspections, he would improvise a prelude and fugue—a musical composition consisting of an introduction and interweaving themes—to test the organ for power and clarity.

When Bach tested the foot pedals on the organ at Cassel, rector Constantin Bellermann described the organist's incredible footwork:

> [Bach] can by the use of his feet alone (while his fingers do either nothing or something else) achieve such an admirable, agitated, and rapid concord of sounds on the church organ that others would seem unable to imitate it even with their fingers. When he was called . . . to Cassel to pronounce an organ properly restored, he ran over the pedals with this same facility, as if his feet had wings, making the organ resound with such fullness, and so penetrate the ears of those present like a thunderbolt, that . . . [the] Prince of Cassel admired him with such astonishment that he drew a ring with a precious stone from his finger and gave it to Bach as soon as the sound had died away. If Bach earned such a gift for the agility of his feet, what,

I ask, would the Prince have given him if he had called his hands into service as well?[8]

Although he traveled from town to town testing organs, Bach remained in the Weimar court orchestra for almost nine years. In 1717, however, when the elderly leader, or kapellmeister, of the duke's orchestra died, Bach expected to be given the job. When he was passed over for the duke's untalented son, Bach bitterly resigned. The duke was so angered over the resignation that he imprisoned the organist. Bach was released after one month, but during his imprisonment, the composer used his time wisely, preparing a cycle

Bach quickly became known as one of the greatest German organists.

of chorale preludes that could be used for an entire year. These were later published as "Orgelbüchlein."

Kapellmeister in Köthen

Bach spent the next five years as kapellmeister for Prince Leopold at the small court of Köthen. The twenty-five-year-old Leopold was a musician and a lover of music who enjoyed Bach's company and provided the organist and his family with a fine set of rooms in the palace.

In this atmosphere, which Bach later described as idyllic, the composer's time was completely devoted to music. He spent his days writing chamber music, violin concertos, keyboard music, and other compositions for solo instruments. He composed six concertos dedicated to Prince Christian Ludwig, margrave of Brandenburg (*margrave* is a title given to a certain type of German aristocrat).

In *J. S. Bach*, humanitarian and musicologist Albert Schweitzer offers his technical description of the *Brandenburg Concertos*, which are among Bach's most famous works:

> In [the Brandenburg Concertos] we often have not one but several groups of solo instruments, that are played off against each other in the development of the movement. The wind instruments are used with the audacity of genius. In the first concerto Bach employs, besides the strings, a wind-ensemble consisting of two horns, three oboes and bassoon; in the second, flute, oboe, trumpet and violin are used as a kind of solo quartet against the body of the strings; in the third he aims at no contrast of timbres [tonal character], but employs three string trios, all constituted in the same way; in the fourth concerto the concertino [set of featured instruments] consists of one violin and two flutes; in the fifth it consists of clavier, flute and violin; in the sixth, Bach employs only the timbre effects to be had from the strings,—two violas, two gambas, and cello.[9]

Prince Leopold had his court musicians accompany him on his travels, and after an extended journey in 1720, Bach returned to Köthen to find that his wife, Maria Barbara, whom he had left in perfect health three months earlier, had died, leaving four motherless children (three children having died previously). Bach channeled the grief and pain of losing his wife into his music, writing and performing cantatas for the prince's birthday and the following New Year's celebration.

To perform Bach's new works, singers were hired from nearby courts. One of these singers, twenty-year-old Anna Magdalena Wilcken, attracted Bach's attention with her fine soprano voice. In December 1721, Anna Magdalena and the thirty-six-year-old widower were married. In the twenty-eight years of happy marriage that followed, the couple had thirteen children, although fewer than half survived childhood.

Meanwhile, Bach's oldest sons were showing great musical talent. To help them learn to play keyboards, Bach wrote a book of twenty-four exercises for them called *The Well-Tempered Clavier.* (In Bach's day, claviers—which were harpsichord-like instruments—were usually only tuned to be played in one key. A well-tempered clavier is one that is in tune in every key, like today's pianos.)

Bach's place in Leopold's court was soon threatened when Leopold married his cousin Princess Friederica, who, according to one account, "was determined to persuade the Prince to give up such 'meaningless' pursuits [as music] with the 'servants.'"[10] This situation proved intolerable for Bach, and he soon began to search for a court that would appreciate his talents.

The Move to Leipzig

When a suitable position became available at St. Thomas's Church in Leipzig, Bach wrote a special cantata and used it to audition for the post. After a fifteen-year stint in Leopold's court, the composer was eager to write church music again. Bach was chosen for the job, and in 1723 he moved to Leipzig, where he would remain for the rest of his life.

Leipzig, with a population of around thirty thousand, was the center of the German printing and publishing industries, an important European trading center, and was the site of a famous university. It was also the center of German culture, with beautiful homes, well-paved streets, a new municipal library, a majestic town hall, and a vibrant social life. The university drew scholars and artists from all over Europe, and the book trade contributed to the city's reputation as an international cultural center.

Bach was in high demand to perform at churches and royal courts.

In his new job as cantor, Bach had to write and perform music each week for Leipzig's four main churches and form choirs composed of choir boys from St. Thomas's for each church. Bach also had to teach the more talented young boys in the school how to play musical instruments. In addition, he had to compose music for town events in which most of the musicians were schoolboys.

Bach was forced to give up the peaceful life dedicated to music that he had followed for so many years in the court of Leopold. His job in Leipzig required him to adhere to a strict schedule dictated by the church. Bach taught singing classes, held cantata rehearsals, oversaw Sunday and weekday services in the churches, and provided choirs for services in a local hospital and a prison.

Bach's house in Leipzig, where he moved in 1723 and remained for the rest of his life.

With all of these performances, a gigantic repertoire was necessary, and amazingly, Bach provided a complete set of cantatas for every Sunday service for more than five years. In addition to his official duties, the composer had an ever-growing family as Anna Magdalena continued to produce one child every other year.

Massive Compositions and Lighthearted Cantatas

In spite of his huge workload, Bach continued to amaze people with his performances, often traveling to nearby towns to give concerts. He also composed some famous works, including *St. John's Passion,* the story of Jesus' Last Supper, trial, and crucifixion, following the narration in the *Gospel of John.*

Three years later, in 1727, Bach wrote another passion, this one based on Matthew's gospel. Both works are theatrical and dramatic. In *St. Matthew's Passion,* there are solo parts for singers representing Jesus, Peter, Pilate, and Judas. A narrator tells the story, and traditional hymns are mixed in between arias (solo vocal pieces). Although the works were relatively well received, Bach brought controversy upon himself in some quarters for making church music sound too much like opera. It was not until the nineteenth century that the genius of these pieces was recognized.

Schweitzer writes about the reception of *St. Matthew's Passion* when it was revived in 1829:

> The audience was transported, not only by the work but also by the fine dynamics of the choir, which were something unusual in those days. Not less powerful was the religious impression made by Bach's music. "The crowded hall looked like a church," writes Fanny Mendelssohn [sister of composer Felix Mendelssohn]. "Every one was filled with the most solemn devotion; one heard only an occasional involuntary [exclamation] that sprang from deep emotion."[11]

The town council of Leipzig, however, was not sufficiently moved by the genius evident in *St. Matthew's Passion* and refused to grant the composer any respite from his duties as cantor. Bach was reprimanded several times for his frequent unauthorized journeys away from Leipzig, for not properly disciplining his choir, and for leaving many of his teaching duties to his overworked assistant.

A page from the score of St. Matthew's Passion.

Although Bach had many responsibilities while working for St. Thomas's, he took on the job as director of a group known as the Collegium Musicum. This group, composed mainly of college students from the nearby university, met every Friday night at a coffeehouse called Zimmermann's. Coffee was a fashionable new drink at the time, and patrons to Zimmermann's had the luck to hear Bach and friends perform for them. This experience was unique in another way: Ordinary people in those days rarely heard classical music outside of church since concerts were usually private affairs, staged only for kings, queens, and aristocrats.

Bach revised some of his secular works for the coffeehouse concerts and also wrote the humorous *Coffee Cantata,* described by David Ewen in *The Complete Book of Classical Music:*

> There are ten sections, beginning with the tenor's admonition to his audience to listen to what has befallen to Herr Schlendrian. . . . And this is what has happened. Schlendrian's daughter, Lieschen, has become addicted to coffee, as Schlendrian himself explains in his aria. . . . Lieschen extols the delights of coffee drinking in an ebullient air. . . . The pros and cons of coffee drinking are then explored in several recitatives and arias. In the ninth section, the tenor explains that Lieschen has no intention of marrying anybody who is not addicted to coffee. . . . The work ends with a . . . commentary by the chorus on the undeniable fact that, since the older folk have a weakness for coffee, they cannot properly deny the drink to girls.[12]

With regular weekly performances, the Collegium Musicum was more than a mere diversion for Bach. Later in his life, in fact, this was the central artistic activity for the composer, with his church work becoming less important. Bach served as director of the group until 1741.

The Later Years

Bach had always been extremely nearsighted. Starting around 1740, the composer's eyes grew weaker, causing a lessening in his productivity. Even so, in his later years Bach wrote some of the most beautiful and intense works of the baroque musical form. In one of his last compositions, *The Art of Fugue,* Bach explored the many complicated ways in which fugues and canons, musical compositions in which melodies are imitated by successive voices, may be used together. As Schweitzer writes, "We do not know which to wonder most—that all of these combinations could be devised by one mind, or that, in spite of the ingenuity of it all, the parts always flow along as naturally and freely."[13]

By the late 1740s, Bach was desperate to restore his vision. He agreed to an operation that turned out badly. "He not only lost his sight," according to a source quoted in Schweitzer, "but his otherwise exceedingly good bodily health was quite undermined by it."[14] The great composer spent his last days in a darkened room, revising his great chorale compositions, dictating the notes of the musical works to a son-in-law who wrote them down.

One morning, Bach's eyes seemed to improve. He could see quite well and the light did not bother him. A few hours later he had a stroke. Bach died on July 28, 1750, at the age of sixty-six.

A poster advertising one of Bach's heavily attended performances.

SEBASTIAN BACH,
geb. 21. März 1685 zu Eisenach.
† 28. Juli 1750 zu Leipzig.

„MATTHÄUS-PASSION" „H-MOLL-MESSE".
„WOHLTEMPERIRTES CLAVIER."

Bach's death was widely mourned, but the greatness of his work was not fully realized until the beginning of the nineteenth century, when Felix Mendelssohn revived *St. Matthew's Passion*. After that, Bach's surviving works were identified and published. Since that time, they have been widely performed across the globe, inspiring audiences in every age.

CHAPTER 2

Wolfgang Amadeus Mozart

In the mid-1700s, the tiny city-state of Salzburg was sandwiched between the country of Austria and neighboring Bavaria in present-day Germany. The court of Salzburg was tiny compared to that of Austria, but the prince-archbishop who ruled the city consistently supported the arts, thereby making the city, according to Mozart biographer Erich Schenk, "a great musical city, cross-fertilized by the influences of such musical centers as Venice, Mantua, and Milan on the one hand, and Vienna and Prague on the other hand. Here the Latin [Italian] and Teutonic [German] tempers met and mingled."[15]

With a long musical history, the thirty-eight-piece court orchestra in Salzburg attracted many fine musicians. One of these men was Leopold Mozart, a composer and violinist. Leopold was married to Anna Maria Mozart, and the couple had seven children, only two of whom survived. The fourth child was a daughter named Maria Anna Walburg Ignatia, called Nannerl. The seventh and last child was a boy, born on January 27, 1756. Leopold believed that the child was a miracle because he was so small and weak it did not seem that he would survive. They called him Wolfgang. His second name was Theophilus, meaning "Loving God," but Wolfgang preferred to use Amadeus, the Latin translation of his middle name.

Wolfgang Amadeus Mozart pictured at four years old.

Wolfgang showed musical talent at an incredibly young age. By time he was three years old, he could plunk out tunes on the piano, and his ears were so sensitive that loud noises would make him physically ill. The boy also had perfect pitch—the ability to name a note simply by hearing it—and at the age of four he was telling court musicians that their violins were a quarter tone out of tune. By that time, according to Mozart's first biographer, Friedrich Schlichtegroll, Wolfgang could learn a minuet in thirty minutes "and then play it perfectly, cleanly, and with the steadiest rhythm."[16]

Wolfgang began composing at six, and Leopold put aside his court career to devote more time to Wolfgang and Nannerl's musical instruction. (Nannerl was also a musical child prodigy, though she was not nearly as gifted as her brother.) Exploiting the talents of child prodigies was in fashion at that time, so Leopold sought to improve his family's finances by taking his brilliant children on a tour of the royal courts of Europe.

Child Phenomenon

From their first trip to the nearby Munich court of Maximilian III in January 1762, the Mozart children were celebrated for their musical talents. The young Wolfgang loved being the center of attention, and the boy made a lasting impression even off the stage. When he met the empress Maria Theresa, according to Leopold, "Wolferl [Wolfgang] jumped on the Empress's lap, threw his arms around her neck, and kissed her good and thoroughly."[17]

After their sensational debut in Munich, offers began to pour in for the child prodigies—along with large sums of money. To take advantage of the situation, Leopold tried to arrange as many concerts as possible. The children were exhibited in royal courts, musical academies, and public concerts across Europe. They traveled to England, France, Germany, Italy, and elsewhere.

The Mozarts played for imperial ministers, archdukes, emperors, and queens. When they were not playing for royalty and nobility, the children performed one- to three-hour concerts at public events, often playing two programs per day. In addition, Wolfgang met many famous musicians of the day, heard all styles of music from the many regions of the continent, and remembered it for use in his later compositions.

To enhance his musical shows, Wolfgang would perform tricks taught to him by his father, such as playing complicated music on

Mozart's father Leopold exploited his children, at times setting up two performances in one day.

first sight, giving demonstrations of his perfect pitch, and playing a clavier keyboard that was covered by a cloth. As a result of his amazing shows, Wolfgang's name was in the news wherever he traveled. An advertisement for his concert for the Academy of Painters in London read,

> We are privileged to introduce to the public the greatest wonder of which Europe and all humanity can boast. This child phenomenon surpasses all imagination, it being difficult to say which is the more admirable, his skill upon the clavier and in reading notes, or his own compositions.[18]

The life of a child star of this magnitude was by no means ordinary, and all the attention at such a young age affected Mozart his entire life. In *The Lives of the Great Composers*, respected music critic Harold C. Schonberg writes,

> Mozart was one of the most exploited child prodigies in the history of music, and he paid the price. Child prodigies seldom grow up to lead normal lives. They develop as children cultivating a specific talent at the expense of all others, most of their time is spent with adults, their general education is neglected, they are overpraised. A warped childhood results, and as often as not this leads to a warped manhood. The

tragedy of Mozart was that he grew up reliant on his father and was unable to meet the demands of society and life. This was generally recognized in his own day.[19]

The strenuous work schedule affected more than Mozart's personality. The composer was often sick. Before he was eight years old he suffered from a series of debilitating illnesses and bouts of arthritis.

Touring Europe

In the eighteenth century, before the invention of railroads, professional musicians traveled thousands of miles across Europe by horse-drawn carriage. The condition of these dirt roads was far from ideal. They were often cut with deep ruts and were dusty in the summer, muddy in the spring, and frozen hard and slippery in the winter. The Mozarts crisscrossed the continent in their own family carriage, but conditions inside the unheated coach were often damp and uncomfortable at best.

In 1763 the Mozart family traveled thousands of miles, leaving Salzburg on June 9 and arriving in Paris on November 18. In between, the children gave concerts in Munich, Augsburg, Ludwigsburg, Schwetzingen, Mainz, Frankfurt, Bonn, Cologne, Brussels, and a dozen other cities.

London was Europe's biggest city and also one of its wealthiest. After nearly five months in Paris, Leopold decided to take his family across the English Channel to play music for England's King George III and Queen Charlotte, both of whom fell in love with Wolfgang.

In July 1764, however, Leopold became ill, and the family moved to a large home in Chelsea so that he could recover. While his father lay nearly dying, Wolfgang composed his first symphony. Nannerl wrote much later that she had to copy the musical notation while her nine-year-old brother composed. He was so absorbed in his writing that at one point he said to his sister, "Remind me that I give the horn plenty to do!"[20]

As the family continued to perform, sickness stalked it at every turn. Nannerl became extremely sick at times, and Wolfgang suffered from various diseases, including typhoid fever. Finally, after three years of traveling the highways of Europe, the family returned to Salzburg in 1766.

Triumph in Italy

The Mozarts did not stay at home for long. Leopold wanted to take advantage of the boy's childhood talents before he grew too

Wolfgang, Nannerl, and Leopold Mozart at the piano. Sickness plagued the Mozart family as they toured Europe, finally forcing them to return to Salzburg in 1766.

old to impress his audiences. After a bout of smallpox in 1767, which left Wolfgang's face pockmarked for the rest of his life, the family went to Milan, Italy.

In Milan, Wolfgang was asked to compose a full-scale opera, and when *Mitridate rè di Ponto* debuted in December 1770, the then-fourteen-year-old Wolfgang also directed it. *Mitridate* was enthusiastically received, as Leopold wrote in a letter to his wife: "God be praised, the first performance of the Opera . . . took place on the 26th amid general applause. . . . Never in living memory was such curiosity over a first Opera to be seen in Milan as this time."[21] After the operatic triumph, the Mozarts visited Pope Clement XIV and Wolfgang was awarded the Order of the Golden Spur, an extremely high honor.

The Mozarts would continue to tour Italy for the next three years, in hopes of finding Wolfgang a permanent job in one of the royal courts. The tours introduced Wolfgang to Italian music and musicians, which proved to be a wonderful addition to his musical education. But he was no longer a child prodigy, and the royalty was not as interested in him as they were when he was young. In 1773 the family reluctantly returned to Salzburg.

In spite of his lack of job offers, Wolfgang wrote extensively during the years on tour. Between 1766 and 1773, he wrote more than twenty symphonies, several string quartets, and three short operas, in addition to concert arias for soprano and several sacred compositions.

Schonberg describes the many talents of Mozart:

There was literally nothing in music he could not do better than anybody else. He could write down a complicated piece while thinking out another piece in his head; or he could think out a complete string quartet and then write out the individual parts before making the full score; or he could read perfectly at sight any music placed before him; or he could hear a long piece of music for the first time and immediately write it out, note for note.[22]

At fourteen, Mozart was losing his appeal as a child prodigy.

Virtuoso for the Archbiship

The next few years in Salzburg were a dull contrast to the excitement of Italy. A new archbishop, Hieronymus von Colloredo, had come to Salzburg. The archbishop hired Mozart as a virtuoso and had little appreciation for his new employee's talents as a composer. Colloredo refused to pay him well and treated him badly. To Mozart, who had known the fame and glamour of the great European capitals, life in Salzburg was miserable. As Schonberg writes, "[Mozart] knew his powers and knew they would be wasted in a provincial city. . . . [He] wanted a patron with the imagination and resources to let him exploit the ideas racing through his head."[23]

In 1774 the elector of Bavaria gave Mozart a chance to break away from his stifling job and to write an opera for the Munich carnival. When it was played, the comic opera *La Finta Giardiniera (The Pretender Gardener)* was a major success. Mozart wrote to Leopold about his triumph:

> My opera was put on yesterday . . . and turned out so well that I cannot possibly describe to Mama the storms of applause. In the first place the whole theater was so jammed full that many people had to be turned away. After every aria there was a regular thunder of clapping and shouts of *Viva maestro!* . . . When the opera was over, during the time when the audience is usually quiet until the ballet begins, we heard nothing but clapping and shouts of "Bravo."[24]

Mozart continued with his position in Salzburg for several more years, but when he turned twenty-one, the composer quit his job and decided to go on another concert tour. Leopold, however, was afraid of losing his own job with the archbishop and so stayed behind.

Rejection and Tragedy

In 1777, in the company of his mother, Mozart traveled to Paris. On the way, he stopped in Mannheim, Germany, where he began an affair with a young soprano name Aloysia Weber, who would later become a great opera singer. For a time, the couple contemplated running off to Italy to be married, a prospect Leopold heard in "amazement and horror," reminding his son that his mission was either to "seek a good and permanent service [with a patron];

31

or, should that plan go awry, to [take yourself] to some large place where large profits are to be found."[25]

After arriving in Paris in March 1778, Mozart met fresh disappointments. Determined to follow his father's advice, the composer paid numerous visits to aristocrats and royalty, but with little success. Mozart wrote to his father that he "spent a good deal of money

Mozart with seventeen-year-old Aloysia Weber. Mozart begged Weber to marry him, but she rejected his proposal.

driving around, often to no purpose," and he found the French very snobbish, "verging on rudeness . . . dreadfully haughty."[26]

By May, Mozart realized that he was going to have great difficulty establishing himself as a composer. Although he composed some beautiful pieces in Paris, he had made enemies of rival musicians who sabotaged his efforts—the sheet music to one piece he had written disappeared before it was performed. He expressed his grief over the incident in a letter to his father: "If there were a place where people had ears, hearts to feel with, and even a spark of understanding of music and taste, I would laugh heartily at such things. But I dwell among idiots and beasts (as far as music is concerned)."[27]

Tragedy struck on July 3 when Mozart's mother suddenly died at the age of fifty-seven. The hardships of travel—staying in unheated rooms, riding in damp carriages, constantly packing and unpacking—had sapped her strength. Mozart, in his loneliness and grief, wrote, "I sit alone in [my] room all day long as if I were under arrest."[28]

Alone for the first time in his life, Mozart returned to Mannheim and begged Aloysia to marry him. But her love had cooled, and she sent Mozart away in disappointment. There was nothing to do but return to Salzburg and take back his old job in the court of the archbishop. In spite of his many rejections, he remained sure of his talents. He wrote to his father, saying, "If the Archbishop would trust me, I should soon make his orchestra famous: of this there is no doubt." And Mozart remained defiant, writing that, in Salzburg, "I shall not be kept to the violin as I used to be. I will no longer be a fiddler. I want to conduct at the clavier and accompany arias."[29]

Productive Years and Unexpected Marriage

Back in the court of Salzburg, Mozart settled in as court organist and began to compose some of the most ingenious, engrossing—and mature—music of his career. From his pen flowed the *Coronation Mass*, the beautiful E-flat Concerto for two pianos, and the equally marvelous *Sinfonia Concertante* for violin, viola, and orchestra. In addition, he received a major commission for the opera *Idomeneo* about the king of ancient Crete who returns home to many problems after fighting the Trojan War.

The success of the opera, which premiered in Munich in 1781, convinced Mozart that he should break with the archbishop, who subjected him to constant insults and humiliations. After a loud argument with Colloredo, whom Mozart called the "Archbooby,"[30] the composer's departure was hastened with a swift "kick in the pants"[31] by the archbishop's secretary.

After his humiliating dismissal, Mozart settled in Vienna with the parents of Aloysia Weber, who lived in the city. In a letter dated December 15, 1781, Mozart wrote to his father that he was about to be married to a Weber—not to Aloysia, but instead to her sister Constanze. He described her by saying, "She is not ugly, but she is far from beautiful. . . . She has no wit but, she has enough good sense to be able to carry out her duties as wife and mother."[32]

Leopold was extremely upset at his son's choice of a bride, who was from a poor family. The couple married in August 1782, and Mozart's relations with Leopold cooled considerably. The marriage seemed to be a happy one—Constanze was a fine singer, and Mozart wrote several pieces of music for her.

Meanwhile, Mozart was finally beginning to earn a good living, although he did not have a steady job. He performed often as a virtuoso pianist and had a number of rich patrons who enjoyed his musical talents. In 1782 Mozart wrote another comic opera, *The Abduction from the Seraglio,* about a Spanish nobleman who rescues his lover from a Turkish harem. The characters were dressed in Turkish costumes, which were considered exotic and exciting at that time, and the opera was an extraordinary success.

Back in Vienna, Mozart continued to write masterpiece after masterpiece. Working with Italian poet and lyricist Lorenzo Da Ponte, Mozart wrote three immortal operas between 1786 and 1790: *The Marriage of Figaro, Don Giovanni,* and *Così fan tutte.* The first two were immediate successes when they were performed in Prague, and Mozart achieved the greatest widespread public acclaim of his career. In 1787 he was appointed chamber composer to Austrian emperor Joseph II. But the pay was disappointing, and Mozart complained bitterly about it in letters to his friends.

Money Problems and New Commissions

In spite of his success as a musician, Mozart was in constant financial difficulty. He spent more money than he earned, lived in costly apartments, and squandered money on expensive parties. He was

continually changing res-
idences, living in eleven
different apartments over
the course of nine years,
often moving when he
could not pay the rent.

Many people during
Mozart's time, and later
in history, attributed his
lack of financial respon-
sibility to the fact that he
was a child prodigy who
never grew up. Biogra-
pher Friedrich Schlichte-
groll wrote in 1793,

For just as this rare
being early became a
man so far as his art
was concerned, he
always remained—
as the impartial ob-
server must say of
him—in almost all
other matters a child.

Mozart married Aloysia's sister Constanze (pictured).

He never learned to rule himself. For domestic order, for sen-
sible management of money, for moderation and wise choice
in pleasures, he had no feeling. He always needed a guiding
hand.[33]

The composer joined the Freemasons, a men's organization
with secret rituals and passwords, writing several pieces of
music for his Grand Lodge. Through the masons, the composer met several well-to-do friends, from whom he repeatedly begged money. To fellow mason Michael Püchberg, he
wrote,

The firm belief that you are my true friend, and that
you know me as an honorable man, encourages me to
open my heart to you completely and to make you the
following request. . . . If, out of love and friendship for
me, you would help me for 1 or 2 years with 1 or 2
thousand guilders [about $2,500 to $5,000 in 1999] at

The letter Mozart wrote to friend and fellow mason Michael Püchberg asking to borrow money.

a suitable rate of interest, you would be doing me the service of a lifetime![34]

Mozart's financial insecurities were compounded when Joseph II died in 1790 and the new emperor, Leopold II, refused to grant the composer's request for a higher-paying job.

Life did improve in 1791, however, when Mozart began to receive money from works that were being published. In addition, he was offered a job as vice kapellmeister at St. Stephen's Cathedral. In July, Constanze had the couple's sixth child, one of only two who survived.

As always, Mozart continued to compose. With the actor Emanuel Schikaneder, a fellow mason, he wrote the comic opera *The Magic Flute*, a fairy tale about a prince who tries to rescue a maiden. The opera features clever tunes, special musical effects, witches, monsters, and other entertainments that made it a stunning success over the course of one hundred first-run performances.

Requiem of a Genius

While writing *The Magic Flute*, two other commissions arrived. One was a requiem mass (a mass for the dead), and the other was a new opera to celebrate the coronation of Leopold II. The second, *La clemenza di Tito*, had to be written within two months. The opportunities were so great that the composer took on the work, which was more than he could possibly complete in such a short time. As Mozart journeyed to Leopold II's coronation, he composed the opera in eighteen days. The classical opera, set in Rome, was not a success.

Back in Vienna, Mozart became ill with exhaustion and fever. As the weather turned cold, he was racked with long bouts of nausea and vomiting. Mozart knew he was in a race with death, trying to finish the requiem before he died. Lying sick in bed, the composer dictated the music as one of his students wrote it down.

On December 4, Mozart called his friends and family into his sickroom. He gave them the manuscript of *Lacrimosa* from the requiem and asked them to join him in singing it. Half way through, Mozart burst into tears. A priest administered the last rites of the church, and at midnight the composer said good-bye to his family. At one o'clock in the morning on December 5, 1791, Wolfgang Amadeus Mozart died at the age of thirty-six.

There was no money for an elaborate funeral. Nasty squalls of rain and snow caused the few who attended the composer's funeral to disperse before the coffin was lowered into the ground in St. Mark's cemetery. As for twenty-eight-year-old Constanze, she was too grief stricken to attend the funeral. With no witnesses present, Mozart was buried in a mass grave, unmarked by a cross or tombstone. To this day, no one knows exactly where the great composer was interred.

With his family joining him, Mozart sang his requiem shortly before his death on December 5, 1791.

After he died, Constanze wrote that her "beloved husband Mozart . . . cannot be forgotten by me or all of Europe."[35] In the years after his death, Constanze got her wish. The world became aware of Mozart's musical genius, realizing that the composer excelled in all forms of music, including opera, symphony, concerto, chamber, vocal, piano, and choral music. By the age of twenty, he was known not only as a virtuoso violinist but also as the best living pianist and organist in Europe and the finest conductor of his time. In his short thirty-six years of life, he wrote more than six hundred extraordinary pieces of music and gave the world a musical legacy that many believe is unsurpassed to this day.

By the nineteenth century, it was apparent to many that Mozart was, in the words of Harold C. Schonberg, "the most perfect, best equipped, and most natural musician the world has ever known."[36]

CHAPTER 3

Ludwig van Beethoven

Ludwig van Beethoven started life in humble surroundings on December 17, 1770, in the city of Bonn in a region of present-day Germany that was then part of the Austrian Empire. His grandfather, also named Ludwig, was the kapellmeister for the elector of Cologne. His father, Johann, was an unremarkable tenor singer who was also employed by the elector. Additionally, Johann was said to be an alcoholic with a violent temper. In *Classical Music for Dummies*, David Pogue and Scott Speck draw this sad parallel: "Like Mozart's dad, Johann tried to turn his son into a famous child prodigy. Unlike Mozart's dad, Johann did it the hard way, by beating his son when prodigyhood was too slow in coming."[37]

Beethoven's mother, Maria Magdalena, was a quiet, pious woman who often tried to shield Ludwig from his father's drunken excesses.

Ludwig van Beethoven's birth home in Bonn, Germany.

Ludwig was deeply attached to her and referred to her as his best friend. Together, Maria and Johann had seven children; however, only three, including Ludwig, survived into adulthood.

Ludwig's musical gifts were apparent at an early age. He first received musical lessons from his father. Inspired by Mozart's success, Ludwig made his first public appearance at a concert in Cologne on March 26, 1778, when he was only seven years old. One of Beethoven's earliest biographers, Alexander Thayer, reprinted the concert advertisement (which shaved a year off Beethoven's age) in *The Life of Ludwig van Beethoven:*

> Today, March 26, 1778, in the musical concert-room in the . . . Electoral Court Tenorist, [Johann van] Beethoven, will have the honor to produce . . . his little son of six years [Ludwig van Beethoven, who will] contribute . . . various clavier concertos and trios. [Johann van Beethoven] flatters himself that he will give complete enjoyment to all ladies and gentlemen, the more since [Ludwig has] had the honor of playing to the greatest delight of the entire Court.[38]

As the young Ludwig showed continuing signs of musical progress, court organist Christian Gottlob Neefe began teaching the boy classical rules of composition. Before long, the boy became Neefe's assistant. When Ludwig was eleven, he even had the honor of directing the elector's theater orchestra when Neefe was away on business. Soon Ludwig was earning his own salary composing short piano pieces for the court.

A Death in the Family and a Rebirth in Vienna

At the age of seventeen, Ludwig journeyed to Vienna, capital of the Austrian Empire, where he was lucky enough to take a few lessons from Mozart, who was a rising star at that time. In one of history's most famous examples of genius recognizing genius, the older composer told his friends about Beethoven: "Keep your eyes on him; some day he will give the world something to talk about."[39]

The exciting trip was cut short when Ludwig heard that his mother was dying of tuberculosis. The depressed

Beethoven's mother Maria died of tuberculosis when he was seventeen years old.

young man returned home to watch his mother, and then his baby sister, die. David Buxton and Sue Lyon detail the negative effect that Maria's death had on Johann van Beethoven in *The Great Composers:*

Composer Joseph Haydn (pictured) was one of Beethoven's teachers.

> With the death of his wife, the last steadying influence of Beethoven's father was removed. The old singer unhesitatingly put the bottle before Ludwig, his two younger brothers and his one-year-old sister. The situation became so bad that by 1789 [Ludwig van] Beethoven was forced to show the mettle that was to stand him in good stead later in life. He went resolutely to his father's employer and demanded—and got—half his father's salary so that the family could be provided for; his father could drink away the rest. In 1792 the old man died. No great grief was felt.[40]

With both of his parents gone, the young Beethoven was driven to make a name for himself. He soon gained the support of several members of the aristocracy as well as other musicians. When the famous composer Joseph Haydn passed through Bonn in 1790, and again in 1792, he had an opportunity to meet the court's newest luminary. Once Haydn heard Beethoven's compositions, he invited him to Vienna, where the young man became Haydn's student.

Vienna was home to the imperial ruling family, called the Habsburgs, whose court had a reputation for encouraging artists, writers, and musicians. As a result, eighteenth-century Vienna was the musical capital of Europe. In addition to the Habsburgs, several other wealthy families also supported musicians, making Vienna the place for talented young composers to begin their careers.

In earlier years, musicians and composers had been treated as mere servants of aristocrats. But Beethoven arrived in Vienna at the beginning of a new era when, because of composers like Mozart and Haydn, music was becoming extremely popular with ordinary citizens and composers were viewed as stars in their own right.

Several Hearts, Several Souls

As Haydn's star pupil, Beethoven met many Viennese aristocrats, and the young man began to make a name for himself playing at fashionable private parties. Beethoven took to improvising—making up the music as he played it—which thrilled his wealthy patrons. In fits of musical passion, Beethoven would smash his hands down on the keyboard so hard that he would break piano strings.

In 1838 Ferdinand Ries, a friend of Beethoven and his first biographer, wrote about the pianist's improvisational style:

> All the artists I ever heard improvise did not come anywhere near the heights reached by Beethoven in his discipline. The wealth of ideas which poured forth, the moods to which he surrendered himself, the variety of interpretation, the complicated challenges which evolved or which he introduced were inexhaustible.[41]

While becoming the most celebrated piano player in Vienna, Beethoven also proved himself to be a worthy concert pianist, playing other people's music as well as his own. He was supported in his endeavors by Prince Karl Lichnowsky, an aristocrat and musician who once studied with Mozart.

And Beethoven was famous for more than just music. His personality was both emotional and unpredictable. In fact, Haydn once said to him, "You give me the impression of a man with several heads, several hearts, and several souls."[42] Beethoven seldom took care of his appearance, and his hair was always wild and unruly. His moods changed constantly, and his friends never knew when a chance remark might be taken the wrong way, sending the pianist into fits of rage.

Beethoven's rash behavior was also obvious in his music. In those days, pianists were pitted against each other in musical duels in front of an audience. Beethoven's rivals were quickly retired in such contests, and many became bitter enemies of the musical ge-

In high demand, Beethoven was the first composer to financially sustain himself as a freelance musician.

nius. After one such musical contest a rival pianist wrote about Beethoven, "Ah, he is no man; he's the devil. He will play me and all of us to death. And how he improvises!"[43]

Although other musicians might have disliked him, the nobility flocked to hear him, and Beethoven's future looked bright. His output of compositions was very high, and he toured often, giving concerts in Prague, at the royal court of Prussia in Berlin, and in other important European cities. With the money he earned, Beethoven was the first composer to be successful as a freelance musician and did not depend on patrons for money. But it was his skill as a pianist, not his gift as a composer, that brought him great fame while still in his twenties.

"[My] Ears Whistle and Buzz"

The turn of the nineteenth century saw a new wave of creativity for Beethoven. In addition to the famous *Pathétique* sonata, the composer wrote five other piano sonatas, three violin sonatas, two cello sonatas, the Trio in B-flat Major, six string quartets, a quintet, additional chamber music, and songs such as the famous

"Adelaide." The year 1800 was also marked by the performance of Beethoven's First Symphony. In 1801 Beethoven wrote the music for the ballet *The Creatures of Prometheus,* which was performed many times in Vienna. Among other works written that year were the piano sonatas 12 and 14. The first is especially known for its third movement, a funeral march often transcribed for orchestras and brass; the second is the famous *Moonlight Sonata.*

The composer spent his summers visiting the estates of the wealthy or staying in pleasant Austrian villages where he could find the peace he needed to continue his fruitful, creative work. Beethoven was often visited by his friend Ferdinand Ries, who would later become his biographer. Ries and Beethoven would often go for walks, leaving at eight o'clock in the morning and not returning until dinnertime.

On one of these long walks, Beethoven confessed to his friend that he was losing his hearing. The two men encountered a shepherd in the forest who was playing on a flute cut from lilac wood. "Beethoven could not hear anything at all and became extremely quiet and gloomy," Ries writes, "even though I repeatedly assured him that I did not hear anything any longer either (which was, however, not the case)."[44]

Beethoven later wrote of his torment in a letter to his friend Franz Wegeler:

> [My] ears whistle and buzz continually day and night. I can say I am living a wretched life; for two years I have avoided almost all social gatherings because it is impossible for me to say to people: "I am deaf." If I belonged to any other profession it would be easier, but in my profession it is an awful state, the more since my enemies, who are not a few, what would they say? In order to give you an idea of this singular deafness of mine I must tell you that in the theatre I must get very close to the orchestra in order to understand the actor. If I am a little distant I do not hear the high tones of the instruments, singers, and if I be but a little farther away I do not hear at all. Frequently I can hear the tones in a low conversation, but not the words, and as soon as anybody shouts, it is intolerable. It seems that in conversation there are people who do not notice my condition at all, attributing it to my absent-mindedness. Heaven knows what will happen to me. . . . I have often cursed my existence. . . . There will be moments in my life when I am the unhappiest of God's creatures.[45]

Even as he begged his friend to tell no one of his deafness, Beethoven wrote about the other afflictions from which he suffered, including nausea and diarrhea, for which he tried many cures. These illnesses, in addition to the onset of deafness, nearly drove Beethoven to suicide. He wrote his will and included these words: "With joy I hasten to meet death. . . . I shall face thee with courage."[46]

The composer's deafness only added suspicion and paranoia to his already irritable disposition. He would often misunderstand a remark or facial expression and accuse friends of disloyalty or conspiracy against him. His hair soon turned gray and his mouth became fixed in the stern frown familiar from portraits and sketches made during that period.

The composer's stubborn nature, however, helped him come to terms with his fate. In another letter to Wegeler, he exhibited his resolve to succeed when he wrote, "I will take Fate by the throat; it shall not wholly overcome me. Oh, it is so beautiful to live—to live a thousand times!"[47]

A Musical Metamorphosis

With his hearing abilities quickly fading, Beethoven knew that his days as a concert pianist were numbered. He began composing in an almost desperate fashion, laying his head on the

As his hearing failed, Beethoven found an outlet for his pain and disappointment in composing.

piano so he could hear the notes, determined to be a master of his own fate. According to Pogue and Speck, by "expressing his pain in music, Beethoven single-handedly took music from the Classical style into the Romantic period, where the most important element in music was the expression of *feelings.*"[48]

In the summer of 1803, Beethoven began work on his third symphony, *Eroica (Heroic),* which was a musical tribute to French ruler Napoléon Bonaparte. Like its subject—who had announced that he was fighting for the rights of the common person—*Eroica* was revolutionary. Twice as long as any symphony by Mozart or Haydn, it contains music that was so innovative for its time—even in places raucous—that audiences at first resisted it.

Beethoven's *Eroica* changed the standard system for writing symphonies and established new musical forms that would be adopted by later composers. Harold C. Schonberg describes the importance of Beethoven's Third Symphony:

> After the turning point of the *Eroica* . . . Beethoven was confident, a master of form, with a fertile mind and an individuality that made its own rules. Under his pen, sonata form underwent a metamorphosis. Beethoven took the sonata form of Haydn and Mozart, and the majority of his great works—the symphonies, concertos, quartets, piano and violin sonatas, trios and other chamber music—are expressed in sonata form, *his* sonata form, not textbook sonata form. . . . Beethoven bent and twisted sonata form to suit himself and his material. His invention and resource never flagged.[49]

For the next several years, Beethoven lived a life of monumental music and heartbreaking love affairs. His compositions grew ever greater while his relationships with women caused commotion in his life. He was constantly in relationships with noblewomen, all of them unavailable for marriage to a commoner like Beethoven. As Wegeler wrote, "Beethoven was always involved in a love affair. . . . Each one of his loves was of much higher social standing than he."[50]

A few of the composer's love interests included Giulietta Guicciardi, to whom he dedicated *Moonlight Sonata.* Another was her cousin Therese von Brunswick, who was his inspiration for *Appassionata Sonata.* A third was fifteen-year-old Therese Malfatti, and a fourth was poet Bettina Branfano. It was probably to one of these women that the composer wrote the remarkable letter entitled "Immortal Beloved," found in a secret drawer after his death. In the letter

Beethoven writes of his tortured distress and emotional intensity: "What tearful longing for you—for you—you—my life—my all. . . . Oh, do continue to love me—never misjudge your lover's most faithful heart. Ever yours, ever mine, ever ours."[51]

Public and Private Battles

Between writing and searching for love, Beethoven had time for public performances. In 1808 he gave a well-attended concert in Vienna, but the program was long, and Beethoven's piano playing suffered because of his deafness. After this disastrous evening, Beethoven began to worry that he could no longer make a living as a concert pianist.

Beethoven's famous love letter "Immortal Beloved."

He almost took a job as senior court musician for the king of Westphalia, but when three Viennese aristocrats combined resources and offered Beethoven a salary for life if he would remain in Vienna, Beethoven gladly accepted.

With financial backing secured, Beethoven created some of his immortal masterpieces in the next four years, including his Fifth and Sixth Symphonies, his Violin Concerto no. 1, and the piano concerto known as *Emperor Concerto*. While his music reached ever greater heights, his personality and appearance reached new lows. He often appeared in public disheveled and dirty, muttering obscure musical passages to himself, and his behavior toward others was suspicious, mean-tempered, and stubborn.

Friends who stood by Beethoven were made to suffer. He drove away one of his dearest friends, Stephan von Breuning, for a misinterpreted casual remark, and this after von Breuning had nursed Beethoven through a serious illness. The composer heaped abuse on fellow musicians who were hired to play his works, and his treatment of service workers has been described as nothing short of cruel: At a noonday meal in a Viennese tavern, Beethoven threw a hot dish of meat and gravy at a waiter who brought him the wrong order.

A new source of anxiety was added to the composer's life in 1815, when his brother Casper Carl died. Beethoven was appointed to joint guardianship of Casper's son, Karl, with the boy's mother, Johanna. Beethoven, who believed Johanna had a "wicked disposition,"[52] immediately began legal proceedings to get sole custody of Karl.

The lawsuit was drawn out for more than eleven years, and the child was "tossed back and forth like a ball"[53] between the two warring parties. During the battle, Beethoven was often extremely abusive to Johanna, who asked, "How can a deaf, madman bachelor guard the boy's welfare?"[54] The stress of the fight added to Beethoven's already unstable physical and mental condition, and the composer did not finally secure custody of Karl until 1820, when the boy was twenty years old.

After the suit was won, however, it hardly seemed worth the effort. Karl was a lazy young man fond of wine, women, and gambling, and he piled up huge debts at his uncle's expense. He treated Beethoven with disrespect and contempt, and he lurched from one crisis to another. Beethoven tried to reform his nephew and win his love until Karl finally found a niche for himself in the army.

In Spite of Deafness, a "Volley of Applause"

Beethoven's battles with Johanna and Karl seemed to sap his creative strength, and for several years the composer wrote very little. In 1818, however, Beethoven's inspiration once again seemed to return to him, and he entered a period of unchecked creativity.

During this time Beethoven wrote his last five great piano sonatas, the monumental thirty-three waltzes for piano known as the *Diabelli Variations,* and the *Missa Solemnis* for soloists, choir, organ, and orchestra. At this time Beethoven also wrote possibly his most famous work, the astounding hour-long Ninth Symphony. Beethoven headed the manuscript with the famous words: "From the heart—may it go to the heart."[55] Schonberg writes, "Here we are on a rarefied plane of music. Nothing like it has been composed, nothing like it can ever again be."[56]

By this time Beethoven was completely deaf. Communications with others had to be written down on paper. Despite this, Beethoven was still desperately trying to conduct orchestras in public. The great soprano Wilhelmine Schröder, who sang in *Fidelio,* Beethoven's only opera, recalls the composer trying to conduct at a rehearsal in 1822:

With a bewildered face and unearthly inspired eyes, waving his baton back and forth with violent motions, [Beethoven] stood in the midst of the performing musicians and didn't hear a note! If he thought [the music] should be [played] *piano* [at low volume] he crouched down almost under the conductor's desk and if he wanted [it played] *forte* [loud and forceful] he jumped up with the strangest gestures, uttering the weirdest sounds. With each piece our courage dwindled further. . . . The inevitable happened: the deaf master

In his lifetime, Beethoven created nine symphonies, five piano concerti, and thirty-two piano sonatas.

threw the singers and orchestra completely off the beat and into the greatest confusion, and no one knew any longer where they were.[57]

The musicians, fearful of Beethoven's wild temper, were afraid to tell the composer the truth. When someone handed him a note that read, "Please do not go on," Beethoven fled the theater, threw himself on the sofa, and covered his face with his hands, "a picture of profound melancholy and depression."[58]

Two years later, the Ninth Symphony was performed in Vienna after only two rehearsals. The theater was not sold out—many box seats were empty, and no one from the court appeared. Beethoven stood on the conductor's podium, but the first violinist, who was the kapellmeister of the orchestra, beat time. When the symphony ended, the audience stood up and broke into wild, enthusiastic applause. Beethoven, whose back was to the audience, could hear none of it and stood sadly at the end of the performance, assuming the audience had not enjoyed it. When one of the soloists turned the master to face the crowd, they showed him their appreciation by throwing their hats into the air and waving their handkerchiefs. Beethoven acknowledged his gratitude with a bow. And, as Beethoven biographer Anton Schindler writes, "This set off an almost unprecedented volley of jubilant applause that went on and on as the joyful listeners sought to express their thanks for the pleasure they had just been granted."[59]

"Not Another Heartbeat More!"

In 1826 Beethoven became ill and was confined to bed with dropsy (now called edema—an excessive internal accumulation of fluid brought on by liver failure). While lying sick in bed, dozens of admirers and fellow composers came to visit him.

At 5:45 P.M. on March 26, 1827, a large clap of thunder rocked Vienna and a flash of lightning filled the room where Beethoven was lying unconscious. A man named Anselm Hüttenbrenner, who was with the composer at that moment, later wrote,

> After this unexpected phenomenon of nature . . . Beethoven opened his eyes, lifted his right hand and looked up several seconds with his fist clenched and a very serious, threatening expression. . . . When he let the raised hand sink to the bed, his eyes closed half-way. . . . Not another breath, not another heartbeat more![60]

The funeral procession through the streets of Vienna several days later attracted twenty thousand people, who came to say good-bye to the man who would later be recognized as the greatest musical genius of the nineteenth century.

Beethoven died on March 26, 1827. Twenty thousand people flooded the streets of Vienna to be a part of his funeral procession.

Although his music was composed at a time when conservative tradition governed classical music, Beethoven shattered these rigid conventions and created works of fervent passion and stunning technical achievement. In doing so, the composer influenced nearly every classical music composer who followed in his wake.

CHAPTER 4

Pyotr Ilich Tchaikovsky

Wealthy countries such as Austria and Germany had centuries-old classical music traditions in which composers such as Mozart and Beethoven made their mark on history. Because of its location and lack of riches, Russia was considered outside of mainstream European fashion. As biographer Harold C. Schonberg writes, at the beginning of the nineteenth century, "[the] entire Western tradition of philosophical thought, culture, and science was largely unknown [in Russia] except to a few enlightened members of the aristocracy. . . . As late as 1850 there was no conservatory of music in all of Russia."[61]

It was into this world that Pyotr (also spelled Piotr) Ilich Tchaikovsky was born on May 7, 1840, in the town of Votkinsk, a mining and manufacturing center in northeastern

Tchaikovsky's birth house in Votkinsk in northeastern Russia.

Russia. The future composer's father, Ilya, a mining engineer, and his mother, Alexandra, were a solidly middle-class couple whose comfortable home was often the center of social gatherings.

Composing at Age Four

Like many other famous classical composers, the young Tchaikovsky exhibited amazing musical talent at an early age. When he was only four years old, Peter (the English spelling of Pyotr) began piano lessons. Soon he had written "Our Mama in Petersburg," a song for his mother who was visiting St. Petersburg. In addition to the piano, the Tchaikovsky household also contained a musical instrument called an orchestrion, which was, according to biographer Herbert Weinstock, "a large music-box provided with stops enabling it to approximate the sounds of several orchestral instruments."[62] By the time he was five, Peter was playing arias on the piano that he had heard played on the orchestrion.

Peter was a nervous, unsociable child, whose erratic behavior was only tempered by music. According to Schonberg, "He was ultrasensitive to music and had a delicate ear. When he heard music—he was taking piano lessons at the age of seven—it stuck in his mind and kept resounding. 'This music! [he cried] This music! Take it away! It's here in my head and won't let me sleep.'"[63]

In 1848 Ilya retired and the Tchaikovsky family moved to St. Petersburg, where Peter attended the Schmelling boarding school. The boy continued his piano lessons but fell ill for six months with a serious attack of measles. For many months during his recovery, doctors forbid him from participating in any physical activities, including playing the piano. When he was well, the family moved to Alapayevsk, but the next year, Alexandra sent her son back to St. Petersburg to attend the School of Jurisprudence, a preparatory institute for boys expected to become lawyers.

His separation from his mother was one of the most traumatic experiences of his life. Peter had to be physically removed from his mother's side to attend school, and according to his governess, Fanny Dürbach, "To the end of his life Pyotr Ilich could not speak of that moment without a shudder of horror."[64]

Two years later young Peter was reunited with his family, which had moved back to St. Petersburg. His happiness was short-lived, though. On June 13, 1854, Alexandra died of cholera. Twenty-five years later, Tchaikovsky recalled, "Her death had a colossal influence on the way things turned out for me. . . . She died quite suddenly of cholera in the full flower of her life. Every moment of that appalling day is as vivid to me as though it were yesterday."[65]

The sad young man continued to attend the School of Jurisprudence until 1859. During this time he studied music and attended the theater and opera as often as possible. At the age of sixteen, Tchaikovsky first heard Mozart's opera *Don Giovanni*, which he wrote "was the first music to have a really shattering effect on me. It took me through into that world of artistic beauty where only the greatest geniuses dwell. It is to Mozart that I am indebted for the fact that I have dedicated my life to music."[66]

Choosing Music

After graduating from school, Tchaikovsky took his first job as a clerk for the Ministry of Justice, a job he despised. During his spare time, he attended music classes at the Russian Musical Society, which would later become the St. Petersburg Conservatory. Tchaikovsky also took composition lessons from a pianist and conductor named Anton Rubinstein, whose musical talent was enhanced by his dramatic physical style and stage presence. In 1863 the young musician joined the conservatory as a full-time student and resigned from his government post.

In 1865 Tchaikovsky wrote *Characteristic Dances,* which was conducted by the famous visiting composer Johann Strauss on August 30. Later that year, Tchaikovsky wrote the Quartet in B-flat and the Overture in F. By the

Tchaikovsky excelled as a teacher at the Moscow Conservatory.

Tchaikovsky moved to Moscow in 1866, but he felt alienated and depressed in the strange city.

end of the year, Rubinstein's brother Nikolay, who was also a pianist, founded the Moscow Conservatory and offered Tchaikovsky a job teaching harmony. The young man accepted the job and moved to Moscow to begin his teaching career in January 1866, living rent-free with Nikolay.

Nikolay attempted to keep his lonely young roommate amused, often giving him tickets to the opera, the theater, and masquerade balls (which Tchaikovsky considered boring). But these efforts were in vain; the former St. Petersburg resident disliked Moscow. On a professional level, the courses taught by Tchaikovsky were going well. In a letter to his sister Sasha, the young man talks about Moscow and his new life there:

> I am beginning to get a bit more used to Moscow although my loneliness sometimes makes me sad. To my surprise, my courses are going extremely well, my nervousness has vanished altogether, and gradually I am beginning even to

look like a professor. My pupils, particularly the female ones, are always telling me how pleased they are and this gratifies me. My depression is going as well, but Moscow is still an alien town and it will be a long time yet before I can start thinking without horror that I will have to stay here for long or even for good.[67]

Frightened Conductor, Famous Composer

Tchaikovsky preferred the solitary life of composing music at home over the social life of Moscow. Between 1866 and 1869, he wrote several orchestral pieces, including his first symphony, *Winter Daydreams* (also known as *Winter Reveries*), and an opera called *The Voyevode*. The overture of the symphony was well received in Moscow when it was played for an official state function.

In January 1868 Tchaikovsky was asked to conduct a public performance of *The Voyevode* at a concert to benefit victims of a widespread winter famine. The occasion was a disaster. Critic Nikolay Kashkin describes Tchaikovsky's debut as a conductor:

He emerged timidly, as though he would have liked to hide or run away. When he mounted the podium, he looked like a man in desperate anguish. He forgot his composition entirely: he did not see the score before him, and gave all the indications at the wrong times. Fortunately, the musicians knew the music so thoroughly that they paid no attention to the wrong indications and got through the dances quite satisfactorily in spite of him. After the concert, Piotr Ilich told me in his fright he had the sensation that his head was going to fall off his shoulders unless he held it tightly in place.[68]

Tchaikovsky's fear of his head falling off was so real, in fact, that he held tightly onto his beard in an attempt to keep his head on his shoulders. After this embarrassing incident, Tchaikovsky would not conduct again in public for another ten years.

The musical life of St. Petersburg—and Russia—at that time was dominated by five men: Mily Balakirev, Aleksandr Borodin, César Cui, Modest Mussorgsky, and Nikolay Rimsky-Korsakov, called "the Mighty Five." Their approval was important to any composer who hoped to achieve success. On a visit to St. Petersburg in 1868, Tchaikovsky visited this powerful group of composers, who gave their blessings to *Winter Daydreams* when it was played for them.

Hoping to capitalize on this success, the first all-Tchaikovsky concert was held on March 16, 1871. With hopes of drawing a large audience, the composer gathered together as many well-known performers as he could. The concert was a huge success with critics as well as with the general audience.

Tchaikovksy's debut as a conductor was disastrous.

In December, Tchaikovsky finally moved out of the home of Nikolay Rubinstein, taking an apartment in a fashionable Moscow neighborhood. Around this time, Tchaikovsky entered a creative period that would enhance his reputation and provide the world with enduring masterpieces. For the next several years the composer wrote his second symphony, based on Ukrainian musical themes and known as the *Little Russian,* and his third symphony, called *Polish*. He also composed the symphonic poem *Fatum* and three operas, of which *Eugene Onegin* is performed today.

A Disastrous Marriage

Despite his growing success as a composer, Tchaikovsky was constantly writing about his loneliness in letters to his sister. At one point he had fallen in love with an opera singer named Désirée Artôt and was considering marrying her. But, according to an account found in *The Great Composers,* "[Nikolay] Rubinstein was among several of his friends who disapproved—probably recognizing that, due to his homosexuality, Tchaikovsky was unlikely to make a satisfactory marriage."[69]

In fact, Tchaikovsky's homosexuality was the cause of much distress for the composer. In Russia at that time, sexual attitudes were extremely conservative, and homosexuality was punishable by exile to a prison camp in the frozen wastelands of Siberia. Although the composer did his best to hide his sexual orientation, there was much gossip among the general public. Tchaikovsky lived in fear that he would be discovered and that the resulting scandal might end his career.

Only a few people outside of the music community knew the composer's secret, including his brother Modest, who was also a homosexual. Out of fear of discovery, Tchaikovsky never acknowledged himself to be a homosexual, only referring to his "inclination" or his "nature." In a letter to Modest, he wrote, "I am aware that my inclinations are the greatest and most unconquerable obstacle to happiness; I must fight my nature with all my strength. . . . I shall do everything possible to marry this year, and . . . shall conquer my old habits once and for all."[70]

In an attempt to conceal his homosexuality, Tchaikovsky decided to marry Antonina Milyukova, a pretty but dim-witted student at the conservatory. The marriage, however, was a huge mistake. As Schonberg observes, Milyukova was "not the mate for a sensitive terrified homosexual."[71] Only two days after the wedding, Tchaikovsky wrote a letter to his brother calling his

Tchaikovsky married Antonina Milyukova as an attempt to hide his homosexuality from a biased society.

marriage a "ghastly spiritual torture."[72] Milyukova, moreover, soon began to indulge in one love affair after another.

In 1877, after nine weeks of marriage, Tchaikovsky attempted to commit suicide by throwing himself into the icy Moscow River. Instead of contracting pneumonia as he had intended, the conductor simply caught a bad cold. His brother Modest took him to St. Petersburg, where the composer had a nervous breakdown. Although the marriage was formally over, Tchaikovsky supported Milyukova for another twelve years. In 1896 she had a mental breakdown and was put in an insane asylum, where she died in 1917.

"You Speak in Your Music"

A woman named Nadejda von Meck was the object of another strange, if more profitable, relationship with Tchaikovsky. Von Meck was a wealthy widow who lived in comfort surrounded by seven of her eleven children and a handful of servants. Tchaikovsky and von Meck began their friendship by exchanging letters. The widow offered large sums of money to the composer to subsidize his art. For some reason, the couple based their relationship on the odd condition that they would never meet in person.

Tchaikovsky was pleased with the offer, and for fourteen years the two exchanged over eleven hundred letters but never spoke to each other. The entire time, Tchaikovsky received six thousand rubles (nearly twenty thousand dollars) a year from von Meck—a considerable sum at that time. And as Catherine Drinker Bowen and Barbara von Meck write in *Beloved Friend*, "To Peter Ilyich, 6,000 [rubles] a year spelled more than riches; it spelled freedom, peace, easement from fear."[73]

Although no one knows why von Meck did not want to meet Tchaikovsky she did write in an early letter, "There was a time when I was very anxious to make your acquaintance; but now, the more you fascinate me, the more I fear your acquaintanceship. I prefer to think of you from afar, to hear you speak in your music and share your feelings through it."[74] The composer replied to von Meck: "I'm not at all surprised that, in spite of your love for my music, you don't want to make my acquaintance. You are afraid you will fail to find in my personality all those qualities with which your idealizing imagination has endowed me."[75]

The two friends never planned to meet each other, but the relationship continued with bizarre twists and turns. In 1878 von

Nadejda von Meck (pictured) was a financial patron of Tchaikovsky.

Meck rented Tchaikovsky an apartment in Florence, Italy, where she was vacationing. The eccentric widow gave the composer a schedule of the times she would be taking her daily walks so that the two would not accidentally run into each other. On several occasions they unexpectedly crossed paths, but they only bowed at each other from afar and continued in opposite directions. The letters from von Meck stopped in 1890, when she declared bankruptcy. She was forced to cut off her stipend to Tchaikovsky, but the composer no longer needed these payments to survive.

Restless Travels

Between 1878 and 1885, while Tchaikovsky continued his bizarre relationship with von Meck, the composer wandered restlessly through Europe, going to Italy, returning to Moscow, visiting Vienna, making his way back to Italy, and then going to Paris. His letters to his family during those years are catalogs of complaints about bad hotels, bad roads, and rude people. From San Remo, on the Italian Riviera, he wrote, "Everything seems disgusting, abhorrent and all I wanted was to die."[76]

All this travel marked a period of very little inspiration for the composer, and he wrote only for paid commissions. His famous *1812 Overture*, written in 1880, was created during this uninspired period. Tchaikovsky had very little love for the piece, saying he had composed it very quickly and that the "Overture will be very loud and noisy, but I wrote it with little warmth or love; therefore it will probably have small artistic worth."[77]

In 1886, when Tchaikovsky's opera *Cherevichki* was to be staged in Moscow, the composer agreed to once again conduct.

Fearing a repeat of his disastrous experience as a conductor in 1868, Tchaikovsky became sick and irritable as the date for the rehearsals drew near. Finally, the composer managed to conduct the rehearsals and the premiere of the opera on January 31, 1887. In a letter to his brother, Tchaikovsky wrote, "I was terrified at the beginning but soon became quite calm."[78] After putting aside his fear of conducting, Tchaikovsky arranged an international conducting tour, appearing in Leipzig, Hamburg, Prague, Paris, and London.

The Ballets

In Tchaikovsky's native Russia, ballet is perhaps the most beloved form of theatrical performance, and Tchaikovsky is

Performers in Tchaikovsky's first ballet, Swan Lake, *found dancing to his music difficult.*

most well known for his splendid ballets. In the 1870s ballet productions in the Russian imperial theaters were magnificent displays of dancing, costumes, and scenery. Tchaikovsky, however, felt that the performances were marred by the music, which was lacking in quality. In 1875 he decided to remedy this by writing the four-act ballet *Swan Lake*. Unfortunately, the composer knew little about ballet production, and his music was not well received by the musicians or the dancers. Weinstock writes, "Sections [of the ballet] were omitted because the [ballet] authorities found them undanceable. . . . It was quite simply more music than ballet dancers . . . could handle."[79] Although *Swan Lake* received mixed reviews when it premiered at Moscow's Bolshoi Theater in March 1877, it has since become a standard in the classical ballet repertoire.

In 1888 Tchaikovsky chose the fairy tale *Sleeping Beauty* as the subject for a ballet. By the time the composition was finished and the stages and costumes were made, the production was said to cost an unheard-of sum of 80,000 rubles (about $250,000). At the premiere in St. Petersburg, the public showed little emotional reaction to the lavish production. Soon, however, word spread about the incredible music, beautiful dancing, and spectacular sets. Those attending later performances were so impressed that the ballet was kept in production on twenty-one of the forty-five nights of the ballet season at the Maryinsky Theater. Today *Sleeping Beauty* is one of the most beloved ballets in the world.

In light of this success, Tchaikovsky decided to compose a one-act opera, called *Yolanta,* which would be performed with a two-act ballet. The ballet was *The Nutcracker,* based on the story "The Nutcracker and the Mouse King" by Amadeus Hoffmann. When *The Nutcracker* premiered, it was met with astounding ovations by the audience, and Tchaikovsky's reputation as a popular, world-class composer was assured.

The American Tour

During the last several years of Tchaikovsky's life, the composer seemed to put many of his personal problems behind him and simply concentrated on his music. In 1885 he composed a symphonic work called *Manfred,* followed by the Fifth Symphony in 1888.

During these years of peak creative output, Tchaikovsky's fame rapidly spread throughout the world. The composer traveled relentlessly to the great capital cities of Europe to conduct "Tchaikovsky Festivals" in front of large crowds. His fame was so widespread, in fact, that in April 1891 Tchaikovsky sailed across the Atlantic to conduct his music at the opening ceremonies for Carnegie Hall in New York City. As always, the composer kept a detailed record of his travels in diaries and letters back home to his family.

Tchaikovsky was much impressed with his friendly reception in New York, the tall buildings in the city, and the money spent to build Carnegie Hall. He described it to his brother:

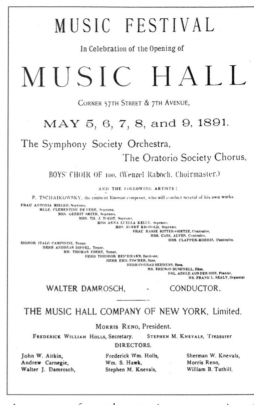

MUSIC FESTIVAL

In Celebration of the Opening of

MUSIC HALL

CORNER 57TH STREET & 7TH AVENUE,

MAY 5, 6, 7, 8, and 9, 1891.

The Symphony Society Orchestra,
The Oratorio Society Chorus,

BOYS' CHOIR OF 100, (Wenzel Raboch, Choirmaster.)

AND THE FOLLOWING ARTISTS :

P. TSCHAIKOWSKY, the eminent Russian composer, who will conduct several of his own works.

FRAU ANTONIA MIELKE, Soprano,
MLLE. CLEMENTINE DEVERE, Soprano,
MRS. GERRIT SMITH, Soprano,
MRS. TH. J. TOEDT, Soprano,
MISS ANNA LUELLA KELLY, Soprano,
MRS. KNORT KRONOLD, Soprano,
FRAU MARIE RITTER-GOETZE, Contralto,
MRS. CARL ALVES, Contralto,
MRS. CLAPPER-MORRIS, Contralto.

SIGNOR ITALO CAMPININI, Tenor,
HERR ANDREAS DIPPEL, Tenor,
MR. THOMAS EBERT, Tenor,
HERR THEODOR REICHMANN, Baritone,
HERR EMIL FISCHER, Bass,
HERR CONRAD BEHRENS, Bass,
MR. ERICSON BUSHNELL, Bass,
FRL. ADELE AUS DER OHE, Pianist,
MR. FRANK L. SEALY, Organist

WALTER DAMROSCH, - CONDUCTOR.

THE MUSIC HALL COMPANY OF NEW YORK, Limited.

MORRIS RENO, President.

FREDERICK WILLIAM HOLLS, Secretary. STEPHEN M. KNEVALS, Treasurer

DIRECTORS.

John W. Aitkin, Frederick Wm. Holls, Sherman W. Knevals,
Andrew Carnegie, Wm. S. Hawk, Morris Reno,
Walter J. Damrosch, Stephen M. Knevals, William B. Tuthill.

A program from the opening ceremonies of Carnegie Hall.

I am a much bigger fish here than in Europe. American life, their customs, their ways—I find all this extraordinarily interesting and novel; and at every turn one comes upon things which are staggeringly impressive in their colossal dimensions by comparison with Europe. The place is bubbling over with life, and though the main interest is profit the Americans are also very attentive to art. Proof of this is the huge [Carnegie Hall] which they have just built and the opening of which was the cause of my being invited here. This building cost millions and it was paid for by music lovers. These wealthy enthusiasts maintain a permanent orchestra. We have nothing like this! I must admit that the scale and impressiveness of all [that] the Americans undertake is tremendously attractive. I also like the comfort about which they take so much trouble. My room, just like every other room in all the hotels, has gas and electric light and a private bathroom and lavatory; there is heaps of extremely comfortable furniture . . . and all sorts of things to make one comfortable which do not exist in Europe. In short, there is a great deal about the country which I like very much and find remarkably interesting.[80]

But in his usual manner, Tchaikovsky found many things to complain about, including the intrusive American press. When a story about him in the newspaper said he was sixty years old (he was fifty-one), the composer became annoyed that the press wrote about him personally instead of his music. But the American public was dazzled by the visitor from Russia. In a letter, Tchaikovsky described to his family how the American public idolized him:

> I have had magnificent success. . . . The press is singing my praises as I never even hoped to be praised in Russia. The ladies collect in crowds during the intervals and at the end of a concert gape at me, and some come up to express their admiration. Everybody is wonderfully kind.[81]

Before returning home to St. Petersburg, Tchaikovsky visited Niagara Falls; Washington, D.C.; and conducted concerts in Philadelphia and Baltimore.

Drinking Bad Water

The last three years of Tchaikovsky's life were filled with the dramatic work of composing his sixth symphony in B minor, known as the *Pathétique*. The composer meant the work to be the crown jewel of his creative career, but he also wrote that he wanted the symphony to be mysterious and tragic, and "an enigma for everybody. Let them puzzle their heads over it."[82]

When the symphony premiered on October 28, 1893, it received a cool reception. Rimsky-Korsakov explained the crowd's reaction: "The public simply had not fathomed [*Pathétique*] the first time, had not paid enough attention to it."[83]

In later years, the public came to love the *Pathétique,* and as critic Schonberg writes, "It is the greatest of his symphonies, and its last movement, which starts with a cry and ends with a moan, is the most unusual and pessimistic he ever wrote."[84]

Perhaps the tragic overtones of the Sixth Symphony were a harbinger of the composer's death. On November 2, 1893,

The desk at which Tchaikovsky wrote the Pathétique *symphony.*

Tchaikovsky fell ill, stricken with indigestion. While waiting for a doctor, the composer poured a glass of water to quench his thirst. Despite a cholera epidemic being spread across St. Petersburg by tainted water, Tchaikovsky ignored warnings to boil the water before drinking it. By that evening, the composer was doubled over with severe cramps, a symptom of cholera. Within days he was delirious and calling out the name of Nadejda von Meck.

Early in the morning of November 6, 1893, the fifty-three-year-old Tchaikovsky died. He was buried in the cemetery of Alexandro-Nevskaya Church four days later.

The entire country of Russia mourned for their native son, and memorial concerts were held in Moscow, St. Petersburg, Kharkhov, and Kiev. As word of his death spread, Tchaikovsky's fame grew to even greater proportions in the United States,

England, Germany, and South America. By the 1920s Tchaikovsky's reputation had surpassed that of all of the other famous Russian composers of the Mighty Five. And the joyous, uplifting—and sometimes sorrowful—musical voice of Pyotr Ilich Tchaikovsky has remained mesmerizing and powerful to this day.

CHAPTER 5

Giacomo Puccini

Operas—theatrical presentations set to music—were first performed by ancient Greeks thousands of years ago. The art form was revived in Italy in the Middle Ages, and by the late sixteenth century, Claudio Monteverdi was writing elaborate operas produced, according to David Pogue and Scott Speck in *Opera for Dummies,* with "moveable scenery pieces, smoke machines, and even roof-mounted harness rigs that made actors fly around the stage."[85]

By the end of the nineteenth century, the popularity of opera had spread across Europe and into North and South America. And the most popular composer of Italian opera was Giacomo Puccini, who wrote four of the most famous operas of all time: *La Bohème, Tosca, Madama Butterfly,* and *Turandot.*

Giacomo Puccini was born in the ancient Italian village of Lucca in the Tuscan region on December 22, 1858. His father, Michele, and mother, Albina Magi, might have guessed that their baby would one day become a famous composer: Giacomo's father, his grandfather, and all of their ancestors—dating back five generations—had all been professional musicians and composers. Giacomo's mother was also a musician. Puccini biographer Mosco Carner elaborates on this unusual situation: "If we were to draw up a statistical list of the great families in which a creative gift for music was hereditary, it would show that the Puccinis, with their five generations, rank immediately after the Bachs, who, with seven generations, represent the record."[86]

Lucca, the Italian village where Giacomo Puccini was born.

Michele Puccini, who had already fathered five daughters, was an honored organist and choirmaster of the city of Lucca as well as a composer of operas, symphonic pieces, and religious works. Unfortunately, Giacomo was not quite six years old when his father died, leaving Albina, who was only thirty-three, with seven children to raise alone. (Giacomo's younger brother, Michele, was born three months after his father's death.)

Appointed to Father's Post

Although Puccini barely remembered his father, he was given something entirely unique a month after the death of his parent. Because of the musical tradition in the Puccini family, the city fathers of Lucca appointed Giacomo to Michele's post as city organist, to begin as soon as the young man was able to perform such duties. Carner writes, "That a six-year-old child should thus be assured of his father's post must be unique in musical history."[87]

The young Giacomo, however, failed at first to live up to expectations. As he grew older, his grades in school were poor, he disliked any sort of work, and he spent most of his hours hunting birds and smoking cigarettes in the fields around Lucca. His role as the organist for Lucca never materialized.

Giacomo's musical instruction was at first left up to his Uncle Fortunato, who taught the boy to play the organ and sing, often kicking the boy in the shins when he sang a wrong note. This punishment stayed with Puccini his entire life. According to biographer Howard Greenfeld, "Puccini was later to attribute his own involuntary jerking of his knee whenever he heard a wrong note to his early training."[88] Seeing that her son was making little progress in his musical studies, Albina sent Giacomo to a new teacher, Carlo Angeloni. Under Angeloni's care, Puccini's interest in music quickly improved, and he was soon serving as a choirboy in two of Lucca's churches.

Although the Puccinis had Michele's small pension to live on, the family was constantly short of funds, and Albina had to sell her husband's books, paintings, and ancient musical scores written by his ancestors to make ends meet. To help his family out of their desperate situation, fourteen-year-old Giacomo found work playing the organ at churches in the region. By the age of sixteen, he was composing some of the religious music that he played. In addition, the young man earned money teaching music to children as well as playing recitals in the homes of Lucca's wealthier citizens.

A Musical Window Opened

Angeloni introduced his student to the operas of Giuseppe Verdi, who was a major star in Italy at that time. Puccini heard his first live opera, Verdi's *Aida,* in a theater on March 11, 1876. At that time, the enthusiastic public reception of *Aida* was similar to the excitement surrounding a modern pop music sensation, and Verdi was earning large sums of money for his theatrical work.

But it was more than material wealth that attracted the seventeen-year-old Puccini to opera. As Mary Jane Phillips-Matz writes in *Opera News,*

> "When I heard *Aida* in Pisa, I felt that a musical window had opened for me," Puccini later recalled. He was particularly impressed by the grandeur of the production, its effectiveness as theater and "the splendor of its harmonies." He added, "Almighty God touched me with His little finger and said: 'Write for the theater—mind you, only for the theater.' And I have obeyed the supreme command."[89]

Once he decided to write opera, Puccini moved to Milan, the opera capital of the world. To aid her son in his studies, Albina wrote a letter to Italy's Queen Margherita di Savoia requesting that her son be granted a three-year royal scholarship to the Conservatory of Milan. Albina's petition was granted, and she called on her husband's cousin, Dr. Nicolao Cerù, to contribute additional funds for Puccini's studies.

As a student in Milan, Puccini lived with little money, enjoying the cultural and artistic center that was nineteenth-century Milan. The young man often attended operas by paying a small amount of money for

Giuseppe Verdi (pictured) profoundly influenced Puccini.

gallery seats, obtaining free tickets from friends, or sneaking in to the theater through a side door.

Puccini graduated from the conservatory in June 1883, and the composition for his final exam was called *Capriccio Sinfonico*. When the piece was played by the student orchestra on July 14, the work was highly praised by one of Italy's most powerful music critics, Filippo Filippi, in the national newspaper *La Perseveranza*. The critic wrote,

> In Puccini there is a decisive and very rare musical temperament. . . . There are no uncertainties or hesitations, and the young composer, once he has taken off, does not lose sight of his ideas. His ideas are strong, clear, and most effective, sustained by variety and the boldness of his harmony.[90]

Filippi was a friend of Verdi and his strong approval of Puccini's work would serve as a valuable introduction to music publishers, conductors, and other powerful people in the music business. In addition to Filippi's glowing review, the professors at the conservatory unanimously voted to give Puccini a bronze medal in appreciation for his work.

The First Operatic Success

At that time the musical business in Milan was dominated by several large music publishers, who financed promising young musicians in hopes that they might someday become famous and thus make money for the publishing company. One such company was Casa Sonzongo, which had announced a countrywide competition for a one-act opera.

To enter the contest, Puccini and a poet named Ferdinando Fontana teamed up to write an opera called *Le willis* (later changed to *Le villi*). Puccini wrote the music for the opera, and Fontana wrote the libretto, or text of the story. The opera was written in such haste to meet the contest deadline that Puccini did not even make a copy of the musical score for himself. *Le villi* did not win a prize, but the well-known musician and musical critic Arrigo Boïto liked the opera so much that he personally raised enough money to have it produced.

When *Le villi* was performed in Milan on May 31, 1884, it was a complete success, with the crowd calling repeatedly for encores. The next day Puccini succinctly summed up the performance in a short telegram to his mother: "Clamorous success. Hopes surpassed. Eighteen calls [for encores]. First finale repeated three times. Am happy. Giacomo."[91]

Greenfeld recorded the effusive praise of the critics after the premiere of *Le villi:*

Puccini wrote the music to his opera Le villi *for a contest.*

> Filippo Filippi, writing in *Perseveranza,* reported: "Puccini to the stars! Enthusiasm for *Le willis!* Applause from everyone, from the entire public, from start to finish. . . ." Marco Sala . . . wrote in *Italia,* "Puccini's opera is, in our opinion, a small and precious masterpiece, from beginning to end." And Antonio Cramola, the critic of the influential [Milan newspaper] *Corriere della Sera,* was equally enthusiastic. . . . "In the music of the young maestro from Lucca there is a freedom of imagination, there are phrases that touch the heart because they must have come from the heart, and there is such elegant and polished craftsmanship."[92]

Within days Puccini and Fontana were called into the offices of Milan's most famous music publisher, Giulio Ricordi, who offered to publish *Le villi.* Ricordi also gave Puccini an allowance of three hundred lira a month for two years as an advance on his next opera, *Edgar.* (Although the opera would not premier for five years, the payments from Ricordi would continue.)

Grief, Scandal, Hunger, and Failure

Puccini's success was tempered by extreme grief when his mother died on July 17, 1884, after a protracted illness. Perhaps because of his deep loneliness, Puccini began a shocking love affair with a woman named Elvira Bonturi, who had two children and was the wife of one of his school friends. When the couple began living together in Milan, Puccini's family and friends in Lucca were outraged. His former benefactor, Nicolao

Cerù, said that the boy had brought disrespect on the family name, and he demanded that the money he lent Puccini for school be repaid with interest.

Puccini's misery was compounded because the money being paid by Ricordi was hardly enough to support the young lovers. Virtually cut off from his family for the first time, Puccini's life was filled with intense poverty and deprivation. The

Puccini and wife Elvira in 1905. Puccini sparked scandal when he began his relationship with Elvira, who was married at the time.

couple lived on beans and onions and would have starved to death if a local restaurant called The Aida did not grant them unlimited credit. Puccini's financial circumstances were further strained by the joyous occasion of the birth of his son Antonio in 1886.

Living under such bleak circumstances prevented work on *Edgar* from proceeding smoothly. When the opera finally premiered in 1889, it was deemed a failure because of a weak libretto. Although the music was praised, Puccini felt that the opera's failure was his fault since he had overseen the entire project. The opera was only performed twice before it was canceled, casting serious doubt on Puccini's future as a composer.

Manon Lescaut

Despite *Edgar*'s failure, Ricordi continued to support Puccini, even as executives in the House of Ricordi demanded that the monthly payments to the composer be stopped. Ricordi offered to repay the money from his own pocket if Puccini failed to deliver a successful opera in the near future.

Fortunately for Ricordi, within weeks of *Edgar*'s closing Puccini had already settled on a new libretto for his next opera—this one based on French author Abbé Prévost's novel about a fickle woman named Manon Lescaut.

Puccini worked on *Manon Lescaut* for two years. During this time his younger brother, Michele, another great musician, died in South America. When Puccini heard the news, he wrote to a friend,

> I am almost a dead man. I could say that I didn't even feel such deep pain at the death of our mother, and yet that was tremendous. What a tragedy! I cannot wait to die myself. . . . Whatever happens to me, honors, glory, satisfactions—all will be meaningless for me now.[93]

Through his tears of grief, Puccini was under extreme pressure to create a work of genius as quickly as possible. Several of Puccini's rivals had written well-received operas, and eighty-year-old Verdi's career was nearing its spectacular end. People were looking for someone to assume Verdi's position as Italy's greatest operatic composer, and Puccini was afraid he might be overlooked. His next opera would decide his fate. To ensure that the libretto for his next opera would be well received, Puccini worked with five different writers to perfect the story.

"The Heir of Verdi"

When *Manon Lescaut* premiered at the Teatro Regio in Turin on February 1, 1893, it was, according to Carner, "received with tremendous enthusiasm, composer and artists taking as many as thirty [curtain] calls."[94]

In the following year, *Manon Lescaut* was presented in cities across Italy and quickly made its way to Russia, Germany, and even Brazil. When the famous Irish playwright and respected music critic George Bernard Shaw said, "Puccini looks to me more like the heir of Verdi than any other of his rivals,"[95] the composer's reputation was cemented in English-speaking countries.

With Puccini's new international fame, money began to pour in. The first thing that he did was order the most expensive meal on the menu at The Aida and pay the restaurant back for the years of credit they had extended to him. Puccini went on a house-buying binge, first purchasing his boyhood home, which had been sold after his mother died. He also bought a villa in the tiny town of Torre del Lago and a large apartment in Milan.

Puccini took very little time to savor his fame and fortune, beginning work on his next opera almost immediately. The composer's next project was to be based on the novel by Henri Murger called *Scenés de la vie de bohème (Scenes of the Bohemian Life)*, a story about "a somewhat romanticized but often honest account of the life of the struggling artists and writers [called bohemians] in Paris of the 1840s."[96] There is little doubt that Puccini closely identified with the bohemians, as he himself lived as a destitute composer with devotion to art but little money until his recent success with *Manon Lescaut*.

Because of his close connection to Murger's story, Puccini was extremely agitated when he learned that his friend and fellow composer Ruggiero Leoncavallo was planning to write an opera based on the same story. Leoncavallo responded that it was he who first suggested the idea to Puccini. Bitter words and accusations followed, some printed in letters to newspapers. Finally, Puccini wrote, "Let him write his music and I will write mine. The public will judge."[97]

Meanwhile, Puccini was in constant battle with his own self-doubt and with the two librettists who were working with him. The opera now known as *La Bohème (The Bohemian Woman)* was finally finished in January 1895, and its premiere in Turin in

Puccini's newfound fortune enabled him to buy several homes. Here, he poses at his villa in Torre del Lago.

February 1896 was a gala performance attended by Italy's royal family as well as by critics from across the country. The public reaction at the first half of the opera was friendly, if not overwhelming, but the notoriously critical Italian audiences spread the word during intermission that the opera was a flop. The next day, critics were incredibly hostile to *La Bohème,* calling the opera a failure.

Despite the reaction of the Turin first-night audience, *La Bohème* went on to play for ovations in Rome, Naples, and Palermo. Soon it premiered in London and Paris, and within five years it achieved amazing success. Now, according to David Pogue and Scott Speck, the "bittersweet tragedy in four acts [is] one of the five best-loved operas in the world."[98]

The Rough Road to Butterfly

Verdi died in 1901, and by that time Puccini had been elevated to his place of honor. Puccini's next opera, *Tosca,* "a violent melodrama in three acts . . . [with] onstage torture, murder, suicide, and betrayal,"[99] was already an international success. The composer himself had become a major celebrity and was irresistible to the press—handsome and dapper in his jaunty straw hat, with his thick black mustache and deep penetrating eyes, and an ever-present cigarette in the corner of his mouth. And while the composer cherished his fame, according to Greenfeld, "the formalities and publicity that went along with that recognition merely embarrassed him."[100]

Left to right: Puccini and librettists Giacosa and Illica during their collaboration on La Bohéme.

Feted and treated like royalty, it was during a trip to England for a performance of *Tosca* that Puccini saw a play called *Madama Butterfly* by American writers David Belasco and John Luther Long. This tragedy about the love a fifteen-year-old Japanese girl (nicknamed "Butterfly") holds for an uncaring U.S. Navy lieutenant soon became the focus for Puccini's operatic talents.

In order to write an opera with strong Japanese themes, Puccini bought Japanese phonograph records and consulted Japanese actress Sada Yacco. Work on *Butterfly* was proceeding slowly in February 1903, when Puccini was involved in a terrible car accident. On a drive to Lucca with Elvira, the composer's chauffeur skidded off of an icy road and the car overturned. At first the chauffeur and Elvira could not find Puccini. Then he was discovered underneath the overturned car nearly unconscious from the fumes of the gas that was pouring out of the ruptured tank.

Fortunately, a doctor lived near the accident site, and the injured composer was taken to his house. A fractured shin was badly set, and it later had to be rebroken and set again. Puccini spent months recuperating and walked with a limp for the rest of his life. Worse yet, during his ongoing treatments, it was discovered that Puccini had a mild form of diabetes.

In a semi-invalid state, the composer resumed work on *Butterfly*. When it was completed, no expense was spared for its first production. Puccini was confident of the opera's success, writing to a friend that he had poured "his heart and soul"[101] into it.

Unfortunately, when the crowd in Milan heard the opera at its premier on February 17, 1904, Ricordi wrote that they reacted with

> growls, shouts, groans, laughter, giggling, [and] the usual single cries of [hiss]. . . . After this pandemonium, throughout which virtually nothing could be heard, the public left the theater as pleased as Punch. Puccini . . . withdrew *Madama Butterfly* and returned to the management the fee for the rights of the production.[102]

Many who witnessed the audience's excess and outrageous negative reaction to *Butterfly* expressed the belief that this was not a spontaneous response but rather one planned by a group of Puccini's enemies and rivals. Puccini himself wrote, "Those cannibals didn't listen to one single note—what a terrible orgy of madmen drunk with hate!"[103]

Although the opening of Madama Butterfly *was ruined by a raucous audience, the play went on to become a huge international success.*

Puccini made some alterations to *Madama Butterfly,* and when it premiered in a small city near Milan on May 28, the audience loved it. As usual, Puccini had the last laugh—the opera went on to play before international audiences and became another repertory essential on the stages of the world's opera houses.

"The End of Opera"

The years after *Madama Butterfly* were probably the unhappiest of Puccini's life. Although he was rich and famous, a series of love affairs had seriously damaged his relationship with Elvira. And he seemed to have trouble settling on a theme for a new opera. He considered Shakespeare's *King Lear,* Oscar Wilde's *Salomé,* and several other well-known stories. But it seemed that Puccini had lost his touch. Fortunately, his past operas, including *Manon* and *La Bohème,* were in continual production in the cultural capitals of the world.

When *Madama Butterfly* played at the Metropolitan Opera House in New York City in 1907, Puccini was invited to New York to oversee the rehearsals. Americans loved *Butterfly,* and Puccini fell in love with America. For his next opera, he decided to go with an American theme. After seeing the play *The Girl of the Golden West,* adapted by David Belasco from a story by nineteenth-century writer Bret Harte, Puccini found his libretto. In December 1910, the opera premiered at the Met. Although critics and the public loved Belasco's *The Girl of the Golden West,* when it was performed in Italian as *La fanciulla del west,* the opera never achieved the popularity of Puccini's earlier operas.

Puccini continued to work on his operas for the next ten years, composing *La rondine* and a series of one-act operas. By this time the Puccini operas were met with mixed success, and none received the lasting acclaim of "the Big Three"—*La Bohème, Tosca,* and *Madama Butterfly.*

By 1922 Puccini was disenchanted with the state of opera in general. He wrote, "By now the public . . . has lost its palate [for new music]. It loves or puts up with illogical music devoid of all sense. Melody is no longer practiced—or if it is, it is vulgar. . . . I . . . believe that this is the end of opera."[104]

Belying these discouraging words, however, Puccini continued compositition on his work in progress, the opera *Turandot.* He never finished the last act. (This work was undertaken by Puccini's friend Franco Alfano, who used notes left by the composer.) Puccini had been a heavy smoker since he was a young boy. By 1924 he had been troubled for years with hacking coughs and sore throats. Doctors found a cancerous tumor on his larynx, but Puccini could not be saved. On November 29, the composer collapsed and died.

When news of Puccini's death reached Rome, a performance of *La Bohème* was in progress. The opera was interrupted, and after

Performance of La Bohéme *at the Royal Opera House in England in 1910.*

the announcement was made to the crowd, the orchestra played Chopin's funeral march while the audience stood to pay their respects to the great man of Italian opera.

The world premiere of *Turandot* in Milan on April 25, 1926, was under the baton of Arturo Toscanini. When the music reached the last note that Puccini had written, the world-famous conductor turned to the audience and said, "Here the master laid down his pen."[105]

CHAPTER 6

George and Ira Gershwin

While the operas of Puccini were attracting international acclaim in the 1890s, millions of Jews in eastern Europe were migrating to New York City, leaving behind the discrimination and anti-Semitism of the Old Country. Among the thousands who settled in New York's Lower East Side were Morris and Rose Bruskin Gershovitz. Like many others who came to the United States at the end of the nineteenth century, the Gershovitzes altered their surname to make it sound more American. They chose *Gershwin*.

The young couple soon had a family—Israel, or Ira, Gershwin was born on December 6, 1896; Jacob, or George, Gershwin

George and Ira Gershwin's parents, Morris and Rose.

was born on September 26, 1898. The Gershwins had two more children as Morris struggled to earn a living on the Lower East Side. According to Charles Schwartz in *Gershwin: His Life and Music,*

> Morris Gershwin . . . was continually changing occupations. Among the diverse businesses—none of which made him financially secure—that he owned or operated were these: bakeries, restaurants, a bookmaking [betting] establishment, Russian and Turkish baths [spas], a summer hotel, a cigar store and pool parlor, and a rooming house. . . . [The] family was frequently moving. Before George had reached the age of eighteen, the Gershwins had lived in twenty-eight residences, twenty-five in Manhattan, and three in Brooklyn.[106]

Although Ira and George Gershwin would become one of the most famous songwriting teams of the twentieth century, the two boys were completely different while growing up. Ira was quiet and studious, preferring books over games. George, on the other hand, was not much of a reader and spent his time in the rough-and-tumble streets of New York, which were brimming with horse-drawn wagons, vendors selling from pushcarts, and roaming gangs of unsupervised children. In school, George was known for his bad grades, his lack of discipline, and for skipping class.

"Peculiar Jumps in the Music"

The Gershwin boys heard little music growing up since the phonograph records of the day were very primitive and radio had not yet been invented. Schwartz writes that young George did hear the music of the streets, such as "the organ-grinder's hand organ . . . [and] the high-pitched, distorted music of the merry-go-round. . . . [And] when he was about six years old Anton Rubinstein's *Melody in F* had made a strong impression on him."[107]

Gershwin heard Rubinstein's piece played on an automated piano called a pianola in a penny arcade. Gershwin later recalled, "The peculiar jumps in the music held me rooted. To this very day I can't hear the tune without picturing myself outside that arcade on One Hundred and Twenty Fifth Street, standing there barefoot and in overalls, drinking it all in."[108]

When Morris Gershwin bought a cheap piano for Ira in 1910, the family was amazed when twelve-year-old George was able to play music that he had taught himself. Ira quickly lost interest in the piano while George began to blaze through music instruction books. George started taking lessons from Charles Hambitzer in 1913, and the new teacher was impressed with his student. Hambitzer wrote in a letter to his sister,

George (left), pictured here with his brother Ira, was a piano prodigy.

> I have a new pupil . . . who will make his mark in music if anybody will. The boy is a genius, without a doubt; he's just crazy about music and can't wait until it's time to take his lesson. No watching the clock for this boy! He wants to go in for this modern stuff, jazz and what not. But I'm not going to let him for a while. I'll see that he gets a firm foundation in the standard music first.[109]

This was no idle praise, particularly since it came from a man whose great-grandfather had been court violinist to the czar of Russia and whose compositions were played by the New York Philharmonic.

Urged on by Hambitzer, George plunged into music full time. He did not write a diary, but he did use an old ledger as a scrapbook. The pages were filled with programs from concerts he had attended, articles on music, and photos of Franz Liszt, Modest Mussorgsky, Richard Wagner, and other well-known classical composers of the time.

Meanwhile, Ira had joined a literary group called Finley Club of New York College. When the club hosted its annual concert for its members, Ira booked his brother George for his first engagement, to play two original numbers.

By the time he was fifteen years old, George had quit school to make his way in the music business. He had nearly four years of piano lessons, but he felt that his talent was the intensive way he listened to music. George explained his listening habits to an interviewer:

I had gone to concerts and listened not only with my ears, but with my nerves, my mind, my heart. I had listened so earnestly that I became saturated with the music. . . . Then I went home and listened in memory. I sat at the piano and repeated the motifs. I was becoming acquainted with that which later I would try to interpret—the soul of the American people.[110]

Tin Pan Alley

In 1910 there were no popular American composers who were thought to be on the level of Italy's Giacomo Puccini or Russia's Tchaikovsky But hundreds of thousands of immigrants were pouring into the United States during those years, and their music was melding with the jazz, ragtime, and rhythm-and-blues music invented by African Americans. The center of this musical mixing was in New York's Tin Pan Alley, where dozens of publishing houses, run mostly by Jewish immigrants from eastern Europe, employed lyricists and composers to write hit songs. (Tin Pan Alley got its nickname because the racket of dozens of people playing pianos in separate offices sounded like tin cooking pans clattering together.)

In the days before radio, business people on Tin Pan Alley made their fortunes hiring composers to write hit songs, which were then published as sheet music. People would buy the scores and play the songs on their own pianos at home or in their musical acts on stage. At that time a type of theater called vaudeville, which offered a variety of short acts such as slapstick comedy, song-and-dance routines, animal acts, and juggling was very popular, and many vaudeville acts used sheet music.

George Gershwin entered this colorful world of music and money when he got a job at the publishing house of Jerome H. Remick and Company. Gershwin was known as a "plugger," a person who sat in a tiny cubicle, repeatedly playing the latest hits for potential buyers. Biographer Isaac Goldberg elaborates on the scene:

The suite of rooms [like those in which Gershwin played, were] known to the trade as the "professional parlors," and here foregathered the fraternity of singers, dancers, actors, and vaudevillians, ever in quest of the new tune to enliven their act. . . .

Tin Pan Alley, where George worked as a teenager.

Whoever has wandered through these precincts at the height of the day's work has thought of one thing only: a madhouse. A dozen singers contending at the same time, in as many cubicles, with as many songs and as many pianists.[111]

At the age of fifteen, George Gershwin was the youngest plugger in Tin Pan Alley and the first ever hired with no prior experience. And at fifteen dollars a week, the young man was earning a good sum for the time. Immersed in the music business as he was, Gershwin could not help but notice the fantastic success of Irving Berlin, whose Tin Pan Alley song "Alexander's Ragtime Band" was a huge hit several years earlier. (Berlin later went on to write such American classics as "God Bless America" and "White Christmas.")

Gershwin was also inspired by Jerome Kern, a composer who became a major star in 1914 after writing the songs for the hit Broadway play *The Girl from Utah*. Kern inspired the young pianist to set his sights on Broadway, and Gershwin later wrote, "Kern was the first composer who made me conscious that most popular music was of inferior quality and that musical-comedy music was made of better material."[112]

As Gershwin sat in his cubicle playing the same songs over and over, he began to add little flourishes and changes to make the songs his own. In his spare time he began to compose tunes that were quickly rejected by the managers at Remick's, who

Jerome Kern, the man who inspired George Gershwin to switch from popular songs to Broadway musicals.

told him, according to Ira, "You're here as pianist, not a writer. We've got plenty of writers under contract."[113] After this rejection, George went to another publishing house and sold them a song about hard-living New York women called "When You Want 'Em You Can't Get 'Em, When You've Got 'Em You Don't Want 'Em." For his efforts, Gershwin was paid a grand total of five dollars.

On to Broadway

As George spent his days plugging on Tin Pan Alley, Ira was honing his writing skills for the show-business market. He often scribbled down one-line jokes, humorous poems, and occasional song lyrics for his brother's melodies. Several of his poems were printed in newspapers, for which Ira was paid one to three dollars. In 1917 Ira was hired as a vaudeville critic for a newspaper called the *Clipper*. The job did not pay anything, but Ira was able to attend vaudeville shows for free and meet some of the performers.

Meanwhile, George was tired of his work on Tin Pan Alley. He managed to get a job as a rehearsal pianist, going over song-and-dance routines with actors who were in the play *Miss 1917*, produced by the famous Florenz Ziegfeld. The play's musical score was by Jerome Kern, and Gershwin's job brought him into daily contact with Kern, who was amazed by the young pianist's talents. After *Miss 1917* closed, Gershwin was hired as a rehearsal pianist for Kern's *Rock-a-Bye-Baby* and the *Ziegfeld Follies of 1918*.

While working in the theater, Gershwin continued to write his own music, and several of his songs were performed in Broadway revues. Irving Berlin, recognizing a talent when he heard one, offered Gershwin a job as his musical secretary for the generous sum of one hundred dollars a week. Berlin warned him, however, "I hope you don't take [the job]. You are too talented to be an arranger and my secretary. If you worked for me you might start writing in my style. . . . You are meant for big things."[114] Gershwin took Berlin's advice and turned down the job.

As Gershwin's reputation grew, he was hired as a songwriter by Max Dreyfus, owner of the publishing company T. B. Harms, which had made a fortune publishing the music of Jerome Kern. Gershwin was paid thirty-five dollars a week and a royalty of three cents for every copy of a Gershwin song sold by the company.

Ira (left) and George (right) sometimes collaborated, with Ira writing lyrics and George putting them to music.

Inspired by his brother's growing success, Ira decided that he, too, would try his hand at songwriting. When George liked one of Ira's song lyrics, he would set it to music and submit it to Dreyfus. But George was not exactly getting rich. Dreyfus only published a few of his songs, and they were mostly ignored.

Things began to change in the autumn of 1918 when a young producer named Alex Aarons asked the twenty-year-old Gershwin to write the entire score for a musical comedy called *La La Lucille*. The show was a success and played for more than one hundred performances. But even bigger things were in store for George Gershwin.

"Swanee" and *Blue Monday* Blues

In October 1919 the Capitol Theater held its grand opening on Broadway. The first week featured a lavish stage show that featured two songs by George Gershwin. The liveliest tune, "Swanee," with words by Irving Caesar and music by Gershwin, was modeled on the nineteenth-century Stephen Foster tune "Swanee River." When it was played at the Capitol, the audience's reaction was lukewarm. But later, Gershwin played it at a party hosted by Broadway singing legend Al Jolson, who fell in love with the piece. And, according to biographer David Ewen,

> When [Jolson] introduced ["Swanee"] at a Sunday night concert at the Winter Garden he brought down the house. . . . The song now caught on, spreading through the coun-

try like contagion. In a year's time it sold over two million records and one million copies of sheet music. Each of the two collaborators earned approximately $10,000 in royalties during the first year, a sum that then represented to each something of a fortune.[115]

Gershwin's growing fame and fortune allowed him to begin to experiment musically. The 1920s were later known as the Jazz Age, and for Gershwin, jazz represented a way to put behind him the simple tunes of Tin Pan Alley while exploring an exciting new musical style. Biographer Edward Jablonski explains jazz music:

> [Jazz] was a form of folk music brought by [African American] bands up the Mississippi River from New Orleans to St. Louis, Chicago, and other cities to the north. Eventually the music and the bands arrived in New York, just before the Twenties began. Jazz was an exciting music; it was often made up on the spur of the moment (improvised) by musicians who did not read music well, or at all. It was music of great vitality and rhythmic drive; it used instruments in ways they had never been used before; it often produced music of great beauty, especially in the melancholy, haunting "blues." Jazz musicians played in a free and easy manner, shifting the beat to the unexpected notes ("syncopation") and playing tones as they felt them and which could not actually be written down. It was an inventive, new and honest kind of music making.[116]

Jazz music attracted Gershwin, and in 1922, after writing scores for several successful Broadway revues, Gershwin decided to write something entirely different: *Blue Monday* was a jazz opera within a Broadway-style production. When it debuted in New Haven, Connecticut, the tragic story set in New York's Harlem neighborhood was well received. In New York, however, the press called it "dismal and stupid."[117] *Blue Monday* closed after only one show.

New American Music

Although *Blue Monday* was a failure, the concept of combining jazz rhythms with classical music continued to fascinate Gershwin. The composer was able to further explore this musical synergism when he played piano for Canadian opera singer Eva Gauthier at a series of concerts called "Recital of Ancient and Modern Music for Voice." The first half of the show featured traditional songs while the second half showcased popular songs, including several of Gershwin's hits. In this first show of its kind, one critic wrote that Gershwin "diversified [the songs] with cross-rhythms; wove them into a pliant and outspringing counterpoint . . . gave character to the measures. . . . He is the beginning of the age of sophisticated jazz."[118]

Gershwin intended to take jazz sophistication to another level. When popular bandleader Paul Whiteman heard Gershwin's *Blue Monday* and his jazz stylings at the Gauthier concert, he suggested that the composer write a major jazz piece for piano and orchestra that could be played in concert halls by symphonies.

Gershwin first imagined writing a "symphonic blues" number. Finally, though, he chose the rhapsody form, which has an irregular structure that allows improvising. "There had been," he explained, "so much chatter about the limitations of jazz. . . . Jazz, they said, had to be in strict time. It had to cling to dance rhythms. I resolved . . . to kill that misconception with one sturdy blow. Inspired by this aim, I set to work composing with unwonted rapidity [uncharacteristically fast]."[119]

George Gershwin combined musical styles in Rhapsody in Blue.

Ira called the new piece, which George had composed in about ten days, *Rhapsody in Blue*. When it was performed by Whiteman's band on February 12, 1924, with George as a pianist, it was, according to Goldberg, "a knockout."[120] Critics raved about Gershwin's new piece, and the *New York Herald* called it "the upper development of American modern music into a high art form."[121]

George Gershwin earned fame and fortune with his wildly successful Rhapsody in Blue.

The record of *Rhapsody in Blue* quickly sold 1 million copies, and according to Ewen, "this was just a trickle compared to the ultimate circulation of the music through the various media. On stage, on screen, on records, over the radio, in the concert hall, in the ballet theater, the Rhapsody has achieved a popularity equaled by few serious works of music before or since."[122] Within ten years, Gershwin had earned a quarter-million dollars from that one piece alone, making him a very wealthy man.

Writing the Hits

George Gershwin quickly became an international superstar, traveling to Europe and becoming friends with Britain's prince of Wales and his cousin Louis Mountbatten. Professionally, George began work scoring the Broadway show *Lady, Be Good!*—working for the first time with words written by Ira. Although the two had worked together sporadically, this was the first time that they had collaborated on the entire score of a play. *Lady, Be Good!* featured the talents of the brother-and-sister dance team of Fred and Adele Astaire, who were friends of the Gershwins. After the success of the play, Fred Astaire went on to become one of the biggest movie stars in history.

For the next several years, the Gershwin brothers honed their talents and became a prolific writing team, collaborating on a series of musical comedies, including *Oh, Kay!* (1926), *Strike Up the Band* and *Funny Face* (1927), *Rosalie* and *Treasure Girl* (1928), and *Show Girl* (1929). In 1930 the musical *Girl Crazy* gave the world the memorable hit "I Got Rhythm" and made a star out of its singer, Ethel Merman.

In 1931 and 1932, the musical *Of Thee I Sing* ran for 441 performances and won George and Ira Gershwin the 1932 Pulitzer Prize.

George spent his time off playing golf, traveling to Europe, and collecting artwork. He bought many paintings by such modern masters as Pablo Picasso and Marc Chagall. Inspired by these artists, the composer tried his hand at painting, with his work attracting the attention of the international art set. As one art critic described his work, "The intense, dynamic impulses of [Gershwin's] music became the dominating force in his painting."[123]

While in Paris in 1928, Gershwin began work on a symphonic poem, *An American in Paris,* which musically described a walk down the Champs-Élysées, complete with the sounds of French taxi horns, music in a café, and church bells. The premiere of the new score took place at Carnegie Hall in December 1928 and featured genuine Paris taxi horns, "imported at great expense for the occasion."[124] Once again, the audiences loved Gershwin's new work, but the critics were less than impressed.

Porgy and Bess

The Dubose Howard novel *Porgy and Bess* is about a crippled African American man named Porgy and his lover, Bess, and their dramatic life in South Carolina. The book was already popular in

A scene from George Gershwin's Broadway play Porgy and Bess.

1934 when George and Ira Gershwin decided to write an opera based on it.

Porgy and Bess may best be described as a folk or jazz opera written in the style of a Broadway musical. George Gershwin finished the opera in 1935; the impressive vocal score filled 560 pages, and the orchestral score was 700 pages long. After six weeks of rehearsals, the opera premiered in Boston on September 30, 1935, four days after George's thirty-seventh birthday. Two weeks later the opera opened in New York.

Once again, Gershwin's stunningly original musical ideas were shot down by critics who failed to appreciate the innovative work. As Goldberg puts it, "The drama critics were overwhelmed by the music, and the music critics by the drama, and both were further alienated by the amalgam of opera and musical comedy that Gershwin preferred to call 'folk opera.'"[125] *Porgy and Bess* closed after only 114 performances and lost seventy thousand dollars.

Stung by critics and tired of life in New York, the Gershwins moved out to Hollywood in 1936 and collaborated on three hit movies: *Shall We Dance?*, *A Damsel in Distress,* and *The Goldwyn Follies.*

Grand Finale

In California, George, who had always had minor digestive problems, was complaining of headaches. At an appearance with the Los Angeles Philharmonic in February 1937, he blacked out while playing a very easy passage in one of his own compositions, missing a few bars of the music. Later, he blundered again and had the sensation of smelling burned rubber. Doctors could find nothing wrong with Gershwin, so they guessed that he was overworked and recommended slowing his busy schedule.

Later in the summer, however, Gershwin began having dizzy spells and terrible headaches. In June he collapsed at the Goldwyn Studios. Again, doctors ran extensive tests but could find nothing wrong. Soon Gershwin's coordination became so bad that he spilled water that he was trying to drink, and on some days he could not play the piano. On Friday, July 9, 1937, Gershwin fell into a coma. An emergency operation revealed that he had a brain tumor. By July 11, Gershwin was dead at the age of thirty-eight.

After his death, Americans realized that they had lost a treasure. Many of the plays that Gershwin had scored were turned into Hollywood films, including *Lady, Be Good!* and *Girl*

Crazy. An American in Paris inspired the famous 1951 Oscar-winning movie starring Gene Kelly. *Porgy and Bess,* with Sidney Poitier and Dorothy Dandridge, was one of the most well-loved movies of the 1950s, and songs from the opera, such as "Summertime," "I Got Plenty of Nothin'," and "It Ain't Necessarily So," became classic American show tunes.

Ira Gershwin lost a brother and a collaborator, but he remained an important, award-winning lyricist for Broadway musicals and movies for the rest of his life. Ira died on August 17, 1983, at the age of eighty-six.

CHAPTER 7

Andrew Lloyd Webber

Andrew Lloyd Webber was born on March 22, 1948, in South Kensington, England. Like many other famous composers before him, Andrew's parents were musicians, and the family household was filled with music. Andrew's mother, Jean, was a singer and violinist at the prestigious London College of Music, where she met Andrew's father, William Southcombe Lloyd Webber.

William was a child prodigy who performed public organ recitals at the age of ten and dreamed of being a composer when he grew up. Although he never realized his dream, William Lloyd Webber did go on to become music director at two well-respected churches as well as professor of composition and harmony at the London College of Music.

Andrew was a fussy baby who screamed and cried all night long so loudly, in fact, that the neighbors constantly complained. The only thing that would calm the child was music. But, according to Michael Walsh in *Andrew Lloyd Webber: His Life and Work,* it was not "the symphonies of Mozart or the operas of Verdi but, of all things, the rumbas of bandleader Edmundo Ros."[126]

Unsurprisingly, Andrew focused on his musical talents at an early age. He started playing violin at the remarkable age of three, around the time that his brother, Julian, was born. (Today Julian Lloyd Webber is one of the world's best-known cellists.) By age six, Andrew was playing piano, but instead of practicing the standard repertory pieces learned by most fledgling pianists, Andrew composed his own music.

"Ear-Blowing Volume"

With two amateur musicians and two professional ones in the house, along with Andrew's deaf grandmother, the Lloyd Webber household was quite noisy. Julian Lloyd Webber describes it:

> [Our home] was chiefly memorable for the astonishing, ear-blowing volume of musical decibels which seemed to burst forth from every room most of the day and night. My father's electric organ, mother's piano, grandmother's

deafening (she was deaf) television, elder brother's astounding piano and French Horn, and my own scrapings on the cello and blowing on the trumpet by themselves would have made the cannon and mortar effects of the *1812 Overture* seem a bit like the aural equivalent of a wet Sunday morning in [a swamp].[127]

Andrew's aunt Viola Johnson was a frequent visitor to this cacophonous household. Aunt Vi, as she was known, was a former actress who took the budding young composer to see musical films like *South Pacific* and theatrical musicals such as *My Fair Lady*.

Aunt Vi also showed Andrew how to build a huge model theater at home, "a marvellous Victorian auditorium with a great stage,"[128] Andrew later recalled. This model was not a toy; it was a real miniature theater with a revolving stage made from an old phonograph turntable. Andrew filled his theater with actors in the form of toy soldiers. Julian moved the little metal men around on the stage while Andrew played piano tunes, staging

Andrew Lloyd Webber was born into a family of musicians. Remarkably, he started composing his own music at age six.

musical plays he had written. At the age of nine, this model theater inspired Andrew to write his first published work, six short pieces called *The Toy Theatre,* published in a music magazine called *Music Teacher.*

"No Ordinary Genius for Music"

The Lloyd Webbers were a happy family but a poor one. As such, Jean Lloyd Webber decided early on that her son should have the best education so that he might become an architect or historian. Andrew, however, had other plans: "I was expected to concentrate on the academic side more. Which, unfortunately, was not the side I wanted; and when I was about eleven or twelve I just decided . . . that I would go and play my own music."[129]

Jean still had hope, however, for her son's academics and in 1960 she scraped together enough money to send Andrew to the expensive Westminster Underschool, an exclusive academy that groomed boys for success among Britain's upper classes. Lloyd Webber was an indifferent student at best, and even those in the music department remembered little about the young musician.

In 1962 Andrew unexpectedly won the Challenge Scholarship to Westminster College, which would pay half of his school fees. This also allowed the fourteen-year-old to move out of his parent's house and live on campus with forty other Queen's Scholars at College House on the campus of Westminster.

Westminster had produced several major British theatrical stars, including John Gielgud, Peter Ustinov, and the pop singing duo Peter and Gordon, which had a number-one record in 1964. Lloyd Webber made the first moves to join his famous schoolmates when he wrote, produced, and composed thirteen songs for the musical called *Play the Fool.* When the play premiered at the Westminster theater on June 30, 1964, everyone was predicting great success for Lloyd Webber. In the playbill, the "Notes on the Producer" read, "Ever since Andrew Lloyd-Webber came to school, it was obvious that here was someone with no ordinary genius for music and theatre."[130]

By this time Lloyd Webber was promoting his music anywhere he could. He contacted agents, sent demonstration tapes to record companies, and played cabaret music at an author's ball during the World Book Fair in London. And in a decision that shocked everyone but Lloyd Webber himself, Andrew won the exhibition scholarship to Magdalen College in Oxford.

The Amazing Technicolor Dreamcoat

In April 1965 Lloyd Webber received a letter from Tim Rice, a lyricist three years his senior. Rice had been given Lloyd Webber's name by a literary agent who suggested that the two work together. Rice wrote to Lloyd Webber, saying that he had heard that he was looking for "a with-it writer," and he had been "writing pop songs for a short while."[131]

Rice, who worked for EMI, one of Britain's most powerful record companies, had never seen a musical and preferred rock and roll to theater songs. He met Lloyd Webber several days after his letter was sent, but it took the two young men six months to get around to writing a song. In spite of this, Lloyd Webber appreciated Rice's talents and soon dropped out of college to write music full time.

The youthful Britons collaborated for two years as Lloyd Webber took the songs to all of the music publishers and record companies in London. In the meantime, they wrote a musical called *The Likes of Us,* which closed after a few performances. The duo also wrote a few pop songs that were recorded by minor artists.

The spirits of the writing team were revived when they were asked to write a fifteen-minute cantata for the end-of-term concert given by a school called Colet Court, which trained singers in the style of the Vienna Boys Choir. The subject of the piece had to be religious, but the song cantata itself could have pop overtones. Previous writers had composed songs with names like "Jonah Man Jazz" and "The Daniel Jazz."

Lloyd Webber and Rice worked on the piece for two months, picking up ideas from a children's book called *The Wonder Book of Bible Stories.* Rice especially liked the story of Joseph and his coat of many colors. When it came time to name the piece, the writers settled on *Joseph and the Amazing Technicolor Dreamcoat.* When it was sung on March 1, 1968, by the Colet Choir, the assembled parents politely applauded, and it was over in fifteen minutes.

No one, it seemed, was amazed by the piece, except Lloyd Webber's father, who asked the boys to expand it to twenty minutes so that it could be performed at Central Hall, Westminster, the church where William was the musical program director.

The collaborators next expanded the work to thirty-five minutes, and this version was performed at St. Paul's Cathedral in London. At the beginning of 1969, Lloyd Webber and Rice were

Lloyd Webber (right) and Tim Rice (left) collaborated on Joseph and the Amazing Technicolor Dreamcoat, Superstar, *and* Evita.

on their way to stardom when Decca released *Joseph* and it sold three thousand copies in the first month. The album was favorably reviewed in every major newspaper in England. Lloyd Webber and Rice were signed to a three-year contract with personal managers who gave them a weekly allowance to continue their musical work.

By 1972, *Joseph* had grown to a one-act, forty-minute, musical play when it made its first professional debut at Edinburgh Festival in Scotland. By 1973 the play had expanded once again into a two-act, two-hour production when it opened at the Albery Theater in London. In 1982 *Joseph* made it to America, playing in several East Coast cities before landing on Broadway.

"Superstar"

The success of *Joseph* still lay ahead in 1969 when Lloyd Webber and Rice began work on their next project. They considered several subjects before settling on a musical about the life of Jesus. Rice later told an interviewer,

> We naturally considered rock [music] with my background and opera with Andrew's knowledge of the classics. Then we had this idea. "Why not combine the two?" [The rock group] the Who had caused quite a stir by calling their [album] *Tommy* a rock opera. That's how it all came about.[132]

An off-Broadway production of the popular Joseph and the Amazing Technicolor Dreamcoat, *with Bill Hutton and Laurie Beechman.*

After achieving their breakthrough success with *Joseph,* the collaborators wanted to continue with a religious theme, so as Walsh writes, "Tim Rice's eventual choice of the name *Jesus Christ Superstar* for his and Andrew's next project was simply good business."[133]

It was, however, a controversial idea to use the name of Jesus in a pop song, and the collaborators were rejected by several record companies before being signed by MCA. When the single from the album, "Superstar," was played on radios around the world in 1969, it generated instant controversy. Letters protesting the glib use of Jesus' name to sell records poured into the offices of Decca, MCA's parent company. The biggest radio station in Arkansas banned not only "Superstar" but also all of Decca's records from its airwaves. Other stations played the single around shows organized with clergymen and teens who discussed the moral implications of combining the Bible with rock and roll.

Eventually the controversy helped generate record sales: People bought the record to hear what the fuss was about. By May 1970 "Superstar" had sold over one hundred thousand copies—a good showing, but not an overwhelming success. In spite of this, MCA officials gave Rice and Lloyd Webber the financial support to write an entire rock opera, or "popera," around "Superstar."

With singers and musicians assembled from various British rock groups, theater companies, and cabaret acts, the ninety-minute double album was finished in July. When the album hit American radio stations in October, "it began a rapid, relentless climb to the top of the American charts, [and] Rice and Lloyd Webber found their lives changed almost overnight."[134]

Australian producer Robert Stigwood heard the album and immediately wanted to finance a stage production of *Jesus Christ Superstar.* Stigwood had made a fortune managing the pop group the Bee Gees and Eric Clapton's band Cream. Rice and Lloyd Webber were quick to sign on with the Australian producer.

By 1971 the double album had sold over 2 million copies, and in July, the first official touring company for *Jesus Christ Superstar* opened in Pittsburgh, Pennsylvania, where it attracted an audience of thirteen thousand. In the first month of the show, it traveled to nineteen cities and grossed more than $1 million. Merchandising and radio-performance rights soon brought in another $1.75 million. The twenty-three-year-old Andrew Lloyd

Webber was a millionaire. As a celebration of his success, he married his longtime girlfriend, Sarah Hugill, in July.

Misses and Hits

By the time the film *Superstar* was released in 1973, the frenzied popularity of the musical had cooled considerably, and the movie garnered disastrous reviews and even worse box-office business. In addition, after working together for nearly ten years, Rice and Lloyd Webber were moving in different directions. Rice had become fascinated with the story of Eva Perón (known as Evita) the widow of Argentine dictator Juan Perón. A seductive radio and film actress before her marriage to the powerful politician, Evita died long before her husband and was elevated to the status of saint by the people of Argentina when she died of cancer at the tragically young age of thirty-seven.

On the other hand, Lloyd Webber wanted to write his next musical about a butler named Jeeves, who had been made famous in the novels of P. G. Wodehouse. The contrast between the fiery Argentinian beauty and the stodgy British manservant could not have been greater, so Lloyd Webber picked a new partner, Alan Ayckbourn, to write *By Jeeves*. When that musical proved to be an unsuccessful fiasco, Lloyd Webber returned to Rice, and together they created *Evita*.

Evita opened to rave reviews in London in 1978. The *Sunday Times* critic wrote,

> The score . . . is an unparalleled fusion of twentieth-century musical experience. Echoes of the past, Tchaikovsky, Puccini, and church choral music, shimmer hauntingly through. But it is the interweaving of pop, rock, jazz, Broadway, Latin, and other elements which make the brew so astonishingly potent.[135]

Evita soon came to America, where it premiered on Broadway in 1979 and ran for 1,567 performances, more than twice as many as *Jesus Christ Superstar*. The production won seven Tony Awards, and the cast record won a Grammy in 1981. The $60-million film, starring pop singer Madonna, was finished in 1996. The movie made over $160 million, and won three Golden Globe Awards and an Academy Award for best song.

Old Possum's Cats

Although *Evita* went on to become a successful musical as the 1980s dawned, Andrew Lloyd Webber was still not exactly a

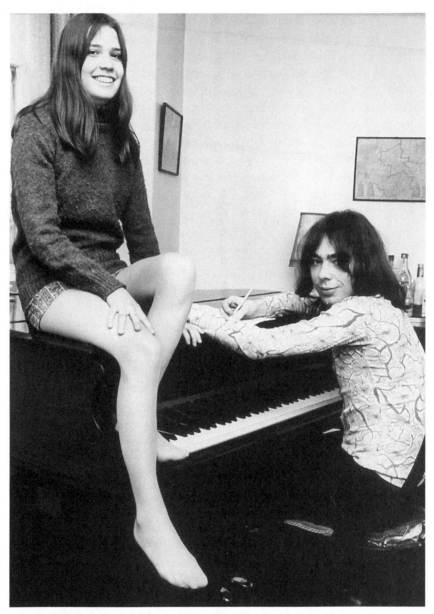

Lloyd Webber married longtime girlfriend Sarah Hugill after becoming a twenty-three-year-old millionaire.

household name. The composer's love of *Old Possum's Book of Practical Cats*, however, would soon change that.

This whimsical 1939 book, containing fourteen poems about hard-living alley cats, had been written by one of the century's most influential literary figures, T. S. Eliot, for his godchildren. Lloyd Webber picked up *Cats* one day in a bookstore at an airport and read the entire book during his flight. As Walsh writes, "They may have been meant as poems for children, but they sounded like song lyrics to [Andrew]."[136]

Lloyd Webber set about writing the music for *Cats* using Eliot's poems for lyrics. The composer knew he had a hit in the making and even put a second mortgage on his home to come up with seventy-five thousand pounds to invest in the play. His efforts were soon rewarded. The success of *Cats* was immediate, and since its premiere, it has surpassed all other musicals. According to the *Cats* homepage on the official Andrew Lloyd Webber website,

> The original production opened at the New London Theatre, in the West End on May 11, 1981. Eight years later it celebrated both its birthday and another important milestone: it had become, after 3,358 performances, the longest running musical in the history of the British theatre. It is also one of the most successful musicals the world has ever seen and has played, and continues to play, to packed houses in approximately 250 cities around the world.[137]

On June 19, 1997, *Cats* became the longest-running show in the history of Broadway with 6,138 performances. The play has continued to sell out each performance, making a profit of over forty-five thousand dollars a week, grossing more than half a billion dollars by 1990 alone. The success of the play transformed Lloyd Webber from a mildly successful composer to a superstar and household name.

Life Changes

In 1982, just as *Cats* was taking Broadway by storm, William Lloyd Webber died at the age of sixty-eight. In honor of his father, Lloyd Webber wrote *Requiem,* a serious style of composition that is only played at funerals.

Then another life-changing event shook up Lloyd Webber's life. In 1983, after nine years of marriage and two children, Lloyd Webber divorced Sarah Hugill. The divorce seemed callous to many, and the British tabloid press had a field day attacking the hugely successful composer for abandoning his wife for a "sexy showgirl who had broken up the Lloyd Webbers' happy family."[138] In spite of the criticism, in 1984 Lloyd Webber married Sarah Brightman, a young singer he had met during the auditions for *Cats.*

In 1997, Cats *became the longest-running Broadway show in history.*

Meanwhile, Lloyd Webber realized his boyhood dream when he bought his very own theater, The Palace. The theater was completely refurbished and reopened with the debut of Lloyd Webber's *Starlight Express* in 1984. Lloyd Webber comments on the play on his website:

> *Starlight Express* started life in 1975 as a sort of Cinderella story which I hoped would be an animated movie. It never got off the ground. Then in 1983 I rewrote it for my children, Imogen and Nicholas, in the version that opened in March 1984. Nine years later we have revised *Starlight Express* whose new music is dedicated to my six-month-old son Alistair.[139]

The Cinderella-like story, which was acted out by trains, was the most expensive musical ever produced at that time. The design for the set consisted of four hundred pages of drawings and used two and a half acres of plywood, sixty tons of steel, six thousand light bulbs, and over seven hundred gallons of paint. In the middle of it all was a roller-skating rink.

Although the show was met with tepid reviews, by April 1991 *Starlight Express* had become the second-longest running musical in London theater history.

Phantom and Beyond

Ever on the outlook for ideas, Lloyd Webber came across a copy of Gaston Leroux's 1910 book *Le Fantôme de l'Opéra (The Phantom of the Opera)* in a used bookstore one day in 1984. The story, which is about a deformed organist who plays beautiful music late at night in a deserted opera house, had been made into several movies, and Lloyd Webber saw the story as something that could be transformed into an elaborate stage production. In addition, the heroine of the story, Christine Daaé, was the perfect part to show off the acting and singing talents of Lloyd Webber's new wife.

The musical opened in October 1986 with Sarah Brightman in the leading role. Like every other Lloyd Webber production of this period, the success of *Phantom* was huge. Since the debut, there has never been an empty seat for the play in the London theater, and the musical sold 99 percent of all available seats wherever it was presented. By the year 2000, *Phantom of the Opera* had played to over 52 million people across the globe, winning seven Tony Awards.

Lloyd Webber continued to compose musical after musical, some more successful than others. The critically acclaimed *Aspects of Love* opened in 1989 but achieved only modest success. In 1993 *Sunset Boulevard* opened on Broadway with $37.5 million in ticket sales—the highest advance in Broadway history. The play closed, however, after a few years. In 1997 *Whistle Down the Wind* premiered on Broadway but soon closed, losing an estimated $15 million.

The little boy who once staged mock plays on a miniature theater in his parents' living room has continued to entertain millions through his hard work and vision. In 1982 Lloyd Webber became the first person in history to have three musicals running in New York and three in London. This achievement continued throughout the 1990s.

In 1991 Lloyd Webber divorced his second wife and

Lloyd Webber with his second wife Sarah Brightman.

Lloyd Webber achieved tremendous success with The Phantom of the Opera. *Every show has been performed to a full house since opening night. Pictured here are the original stars, Michael Crawford and Sarah Brightman.*

married Madeline Gurdon. The following year, he was knighted by Queen Elizabeth II for his services to the arts. In 1997 Lloyd Webber was admitted to Britain's House of Lords as Lord Lloyd Webber of Sydmonton. Lord Lloyd Webber has accumulated prestigious prizes on both sides of the Atlantic: His U.S. awards include six Tonys and three Grammys, and his native country has honored him with four Drama Desk Awards and five Laurence Olivier Awards.

NOTES

Introduction: Music from the Heart to the Heart

1. Quoted in Ates Orga, *Beethoven: His Life and Times*. Neptune City, NJ: Paganiniana, 1980, p. 153.

Chapter 1: Johann Sebastian Bach

2. Hans T. David and Arthur Mendel, eds., *The Bach Reader*. New York: W. W. Norton, 1966, p. 21.

3. Quoted in Charles Sanford Terry, *Johann Sebastian Bach*. London: Oxford University Press, 1972, p. 66.

4. Quoted in David and Mendel, *The Bach Reader*, p. 33.

5. Quoted in Terry, *Johann Sebastian Bach*, p. 70.

6. Quoted in David and Mendel, *The Bach Reader*, p. 55.

7. Quoted in Terry, *Johann Sebastian Bach*, p. 83.

8. Quoted in David and Mendel, *The Bach Reader*, p. 236.

9. Albert Schweitzer, *J. S. Bach*, vol. 1. New York: Dover, 1966, p. 407.

10. David Buxton and Sue Lyon, eds., *The Great Composers*, vol. 5. New York: Marshall Cavendish, 1987, p. 29.

11. Schweitzer, *J. S. Bach*, vol. 1, pp. 242–43.

12. David Ewen, *The Complete Book of Classical Music*. Englewood Cliffs, NJ: Prentice-Hall, 1965, p. 103.

13. Schweitzer, *J. S. Bach*, vol. 1, p. 427.

14. Quoted in Schweitzer, *J. S. Bach*, vol. 1, p. 223.

Chapter 2: Wolfgang Amadeus Mozart

15. Erich Schenk, *Mozart and His Times*. New York: Knopf, 1959, p. 4.

16. Quoted in Alfred Einstein, *Mozart: His Character and His Work*. New York: Oxford University Press, 1945, p. 24.

17. Quoted in Schenk, *Mozart and His Times*, p. 42.

18. Quoted in Schenk, *Mozart and His Times*, p. 72.

19. Harold C. Schonberg, *The Lives of the Great Composers*. New York: W. W. Norton, 1981, p. 95.

20. Quoted in Marcia Davenport, *Mozart*. New York: Scribner's, 1932, p. 42.

21. Quoted in Hans Gal, ed., *The Musician's World*. New York: Arco, 1965, p. 70.

22. Schonberg, *The Lives of the Great Composers*, p. 94.

23. Schonberg, *The Lives of the Great Composers*, p. 99.

24. Quoted in Schenk, *Mozart and His Times*, p. 158.

25. Quoted in Gal, *The Musician's World*, p. 76.

26. Quoted in Schenk, *Mozart and His Times*, p. 236.

27. Quoted in Schenk, *Mozart and His Times*, p. 238.

28. Quoted in Schenk, *Mozart and His Times*, p. 239.

29. Quoted in Schonberg, *The Lives of the Great Composers*, p. 100.

30. Quoted in Gal, *The Musician's World*, p. 89.

31. Quoted in Gal, *The Musician's World*, p. 89.

32. Quoted in Gal, *The Musician's World*, p. 97.

33. Quoted in Schonberg, *The Lives of the Great Composers*, p. 95.

34. Quoted in Gal, *The Musician's World*, p. 105.

35. Quoted in Schenk, *Mozart and His Times*, p. 446.

36. Schonberg, *The Lives of the Great Composers*, p. 109.

Chapter 3: Ludwig van Beethoven

37. David Pogue and Scott Speck, *Classical Music for Dummies*. Chicago: IDG Books Worldwide, 1997, p. 34.

38. Quoted in Alexander Thayer, *The Life of Ludwig van Beethoven*, vol. 1. Ann Arbor, MI: University Microfilms International, 1989, p. 59.

39. Quoted in O. G. Sonneck, ed., *Beethoven: Impressions by His Contemporaries*. New York: Dover, 1967, p. 11.

40. Buxton and Lyon, *The Great Composers*, vol. 2, p. 9.

41. Franz Wegeler and Ferdinand Ries, *Beethoven Remembered*. Arlington, VA: Great Oceans, 1987, p. 88.

42. Quoted in Buxton and Lyon, *The Great Composers*, vol. 2, p. 17.

43. Quoted in Thayer, *The Life of Ludwig van Beethoven*, vol. 1, p. 152.

44. Wegeler and Ries, *Beethoven Remembered*, p. 86.

45. Quoted in Thayer, *The Life of Ludwig van Beethoven*, vol. 1, p. 300.

46. Quoted in Buxton and Lyon, *The Great Composers*, vol. 2, p. 11.

47. Quoted in Thayer, *The Life of Ludwig van Beethoven*, vol. 1, p. 303.

48. Pogue and Speck, *Classical Music for Dummies*, p. 35.

49. Schonberg, *The Lives of the Great Composers*, p. 120.

50. Wegeler and Ries, *Beethoven Remembered*, pp. 43–44.

51. Quoted in Orga, *Beethoven*, p. 105.

52. Quoted in Thayer, *The Life of Ludwig van Beethoven*, vol. 3, p. 3.

53. Quoted in Thayer, *The Life of Ludwig van Beethoven*, vol. 1, p. 8.

54. Quoted in Buxton and Lyon, *The Great Composers*, vol. 2, p. 13.

55. Quoted in Orga, *Beethoven*, p. 153.

56. Schonberg, *The Lives of the Great Composers*, p. 121.

57. Quoted in Orga, *Beethoven*, p. 146.

58. Quoted in Orga, *Beethoven*, p. 146.

59. Quoted in Orga, *Beethoven*, p. 157.

60. Quoted in Thayer, *The Life of Ludwig van Beethoven*, vol. 3, p. 300.

Chapter 4: Piotr Ilich Tchaikovsky

61. Schonberg, *The Lives of the Great Composers*, p. 356.

62. Herbert Weinstock, *Tchaikovsky*. New York: Knopf, 1959, p. 12.

63. Schonberg, *The Lives of the Great Composers*, pp. 378–79.

64. Quoted in Alexander Orlova, *Tchaikovsky: A Self-Portrait*. New York: Oxford University Press, 1990, p. 5.

65. Quoted in Orlova, *Tchaikovsky*, pp. 4–5.

66. Quoted in Orlova, *Tchaikovsky*, pp. 6–7.

67. Quoted in Orlova, *Tchaikovsky*, p. 15.

68. Quoted in Weinstock, *Tchaikovsky*, p. 56.

69. Buxton and Lyon, *The Great Composers*, vol. 3, p. 8.

70. Quoted in Catherine Drinker Bowen and Barbara von Meck, *"Beloved Friend."* Boston: Little, Brown, 1937, p. 86.

71. Schonberg, *The Lives of the Great Composers,* p. 380.

72. Quoted in Bowen and von Meck, *"Beloved Friend,"* p. 106.

73. Bowen and von Meck, *"Beloved Friend,"* p. 142.

74. Quoted in Schonberg, *The Lives of the Great Composers,* p. 381.

75. Quoted in Schonberg, *The Lives of the Great Composers,* p. 381.

76. Quoted in Orlova, *Tchaikovsky,* p. 134.

77. Quoted in Weinstock, *Tchaikovsky,* p. 224.

78. Piotr Ilich Tchaikovsky, *Letters to His Family: An Autobiography.* New York: Stein and Day, 1981, p. 372.

79. Weinstock, *Tchaikovsky,* p. 128.

80. Tchaikovsky, *Letters to His Family,* p. 381.

81. Tchaikovsky, *Letters to His Family,* p. 383.

82. Quoted in Schonberg, *The Lives of the Great Composers,* p. 387.

83. Quoted in Weinstock, *Tchaikovsky,* p. 361.

84. Schonberg, *The Lives of the Great Composers,* p. 388.

Chapter 5: Giacomo Puccini

85. David Pogue and Scott Speck, *Opera for Dummies.* Chicago: IDG Books Worldwide, 1997, p. 58.

86. Mosco Carner, *Puccini.* New York: Holmes & Meier, 1974, p. 7.

87. Carner, *Puccini,* p. 16.

88. Howard Greenfeld, *Puccini.* New York: G. P. Putnam's Sons, 1980, p. 19.

89. Mary Jane Phillips-Matz, "Verdi's Heir," *Opera News,* March 2, 1996, p. 12.

90. Quoted in Greenfeld, *Puccini,* p. 32.

91. Quoted in Stanley Jackson, *Monsieur Butterfly.* New York: Stein and Day, 1974, p. 25.

92. Greenfeld, *Puccini,* p. 39.

93. Quoted in Greenfeld, *Puccini,* p. 59.

94. Carner, *Puccini,* p. 63.

95. Quoted in Carner, *Puccini,* p. 64.

96. Greenfeld, *Puccini,* p. 76.

97. Quoted in Greenfeld, *Puccini,* p. 77.

98. Pogue and Speck, *Opera for Dummies,* p. 197.

99. Pogue and Speck, *Opera for Dummies,* p. 274.

100. Greenfeld, *Puccini,* p. 107.

101. Quoted in Carner, *Puccini,* p. 138.

102. Quoted in Carner, *Puccini,* p. 139.

103. Quoted in Carner, *Puccini,* p. 141.

104. Quoted in Schonberg, *The Lives of the Great Composers,* p. 432.

105. Quoted in Schonberg, *The Lives of the Great Composers,* p. 433.

Chapter 6: George and Ira Gershwin

106. Charles Schwartz, *Gershwin: His Life and Music.* Indianapolis: Bobbs-Merrill, 1973, p. 5.

107. Schwartz, *Gershwin,* p. 12.

108. Quoted in Isaac Goldberg, *Gershwin: A Study in American Music.* New York: Frederick Ungar, 1958, p. 54.

109. Quoted in Goldberg, *Gershwin,* p. 61.

110. Quoted in Goldberg, *Gershwin,* p. 67.

111. Goldberg, *Gershwin,* p. 72.

112. Quoted in Goldberg, *Gershwin,* p. 81.

113. Quoted in Joan Peyser, *The Memory of All That,* New York: Simon & Schuster, 1993, p. 32.

114. Quoted in David Ewen, *George Gershwin: His Journey to Greatness.* New York: Ungar, 1986, p. 46.

115. Ewen, *George Gershwin,* p. 57.

116. Edward Jablonski, *Gershwin.* New York: G. P. Putnam's Sons, 1962, p. 52.

117. Quoted in Goldberg, *Gershwin,* p. 122.

118. Quoted in Goldberg, *Gershwin,* p. 131.

119. Quoted in Ewen, *George Gershwin,* p. 75.

120. Goldberg, *Gershwin,* p. 148.

121. Quoted in Goldberg, *Gershwin,* p. 150.

122. Ewen, *George Gershwin,* p. 82.

123. Quoted in Ewen, *George Gershwin,* p. 156.

124. Goldberg, *Gershwin,* p. 234.

125. Goldberg, *Gershwin,* p. 327.

Chapter 7: Andrew Lloyd Webber

126. Michael Walsh, *Andrew Lloyd Webber: His Life and Work.* New York: Harry N. Abrams, 1989, p. 25.

127. Quoted in Walsh, *Andrew Lloyd Webber,* pp. 26–27.

128. Quoted in Gerald McKnight, *Andrew Lloyd Webber.* New York: St. Martin's, 1984, p. 31.

129. Quoted in McKnight, *Andrew Lloyd Webber,* p. 30.

130. Quoted in Walsh, *Andrew Lloyd Webber,* p. 30.

131. Quoted in Walsh, *Andrew Lloyd Webber,* p. 32.

132. Quoted in Ellis Nassour and Richard Broderick, *Rock Opera.* New York: Hawthorn Books, 1973, p. 21.

133. Walsh, *Andrew Lloyd Webber,* p. 61.

134. Walsh, *Andrew Lloyd Webber,* p. 71.

135. Quoted in McKnight, *Andrew Lloyd Webber,* p. 168.

136. Walsh, *Andrew Lloyd Webber,* p. 116.

137. *Cats* homepage, 1996, www.reallyuseful.com/Cats/index.html.

138. Walsh, *Andrew Lloyd Webber,* p. 155.

139. *Starlight Express* homepage, 1996. www.reallyuseful.com/Starlight/index.html.

David Buxton and Sue Lyon, eds., *The Great Composers*, Vols. 2 and 5. New York: Marshall Cavendish, 1987. Part of a series of books written in England about famous composers, their lives, and times. Volume 2, which is about Ludwig van Beethoven, also features listeners' guides for famous works and many interesting pictures, sidebars, and musical information. Volume 5 is full of biographical, musical, and background notes about Johann Sebastian Bach.

Andrew Lloyd Webber, *"Cats."* San Diego: Harcourt Brace Jovanovich, 1983. A big, colorful book with the libretto, or story, from the musical *Cats* and featuring the poems from *Old Possum's Book of Practical Cats* by T. S. Eliot, on which the play is based.

Don Nardo, *Mozart*. San Diego: Lucent Books, 1997. Some people believe Mozart was poisoned by his enemies and this book explores several theories surrounding the composer's death.

George C. Perry, *The Complete "Phantom of the Opera."* New York: Henry Holt, 1991. The libretto of the musical by Andrew Lloyd Webber, with many pictures of the stage production.

David Pogue and Scott Speck, *Classical Music for Dummies*. Chicago: IDG Books Worldwide, 1997. This informative book with the funny name explores the history of classical music, the lives of composers, the workings of symphony orchestras, and other information. The authors are both Yale graduates who have worked in major musical productions—Pogue on Broadway, Speck as a conductor. The book comes with a very informative CD.

———, *Opera for Dummies*. Chicago: IDG Books Worldwide, 1997. Another in the Dummies series, this one exploring every aspect of opera, including history, composers, and over fifty story lines to famous operas. Written in an amusing and easy-to-understand format.

Roland Vernon, *Introducing Beethoven*. Parsippany, NJ: Silver Burdett, 1996. One of a series of books written in England about the influences and historical events that shaped the life of Ludwig van Beethoven. Illustrated in full color with many sidebars about other important cultural events of the time.

———, *Introducing Mozart*. Parsippany, NJ: Silver Burdett, 1996. Another book by Vernon that details the life and times of Wolfgang Amadeus Mozart.

Michael Walsh, *Andrew Lloyd Webber: His Life and Work*. New York: Harry N. Abrams, 1989. An oversized book filled with biographical information about Andrew Lloyd Webber written by a *Time* magazine music critic. It includes 130 photos, including performance shots of his plays, costume designs, sets, and more.

Franz Wegeler and Ferdinand Ries, *Beethoven Remembered*. Arlington, VA: Great Oceans, 1987. A fascinating and entertaining book—and one of the first biographies—about Ludwig van Beethoven, originally published in 1838. Contains personal memories, original letters, and other interesting information. Wegeler knew the composer from his earliest years and was a close friend his entire life. Ries was a student, protégé, and friend of Beethoven from the time the composer was thirty-one. Originally written in German, this book was not available in English until 1987.

Opal Wheeler, *Peter Tschaikovsky and the "Nutcracker Ballet."* New York: Dutton, 1959. A book about Tchaikovsky's life and times that focuses on his creation of the *Nutcracker,* one of the world's most famous ballets.

Websites

There are dozens of websites devoted to the composers in this book. They may be found by typing the individual composer's name in various search engines such as Yahoo (www.yahoo.com) and Alta Vista (www.altavista.com/).

Bach Central Station (www.jsbach.net/bcs/). A detailed directory maintained by David J. Grossman of J. S. Bach Resources that includes an index with links to 315 sites with information on Bach's biography, recordings, instruments, and Bach-related events.

The Beethoven Experience (www.geocities.com/Vienna/Strasse/2914/beethoven/). This site concerning Beethoven has biographical information as well as the history and descriptions of many of the great composer's works, including his symphonies, piano concertos, and more. Also included are pictures of Beethoven as well as recommended recordings.

George Gershwin: A Tribute to America's Greatest Composer (www.ffaire.com/gershwin/). Highlights of the life and times of George Gershwin with descriptions and histories of some of his major works, including *Rhapsody in Blue, Porgy and Bess,* and others.

The Mozart Project (www.frontiernet.net/~sboerner/mozart/). A detailed site maintained by Steve Boerner that is dedicated to Mozart and includes biographical information, a listing of all of the composer's works, essays about Mozart by famous writers, and links to related sites.

Pyotr Ilich Tchaikovsky (www.geocities.com/Vienna/5648/Tchaikovsky. htm). A website dedicated to Tchaikovsky featuring information about his personal life, his family tree, a comprehensive calendar of his life, and links to other sites.

Andrew Lloyd Webber (www.reallyuseful.com/home/). This is the official Lloyd Webber website with links to pages of detailed information about all of his plays, including *Cats, Sunset Boulevard, The Phantom of the Opera,* and more. Includes latest touring news, cast changes, press releases, and ticket availability. Includes the homepages for all of Lloyd Webber's plays, including *Cats* (www.reallyuseful.com/Cats/index.html) and *Starlight Express* (www.reallyuseful.com/Starlight/index.html).

Works Consulted

Catherine Drinker Bowen and Barbara von Meck, *"Beloved Friend."* Boston: Little, Brown, 1937. For fourteen years, Pyotr Tchaikovsky exchanged more than eleven hundred letters with Nadejda von Meck, a woman he never met. In 1937, the author of this book published some of these letters and tied them together with a biography about the composer. Barbara von Meck is the wife of one of Nadejda's grandsons.

Mosco Carner, *Puccini*. New York: Holmes & Meier, 1974. This book was first published in 1958 and represents a definitive biography of opera composer Giacomo Puccini. The first section of the book focuses on the facts of Puccini's life, the second half on his psychological makeup, and the third on his music, including the plots of his operas.

Marcia Davenport, *Mozart*. New York: Scribner's, 1932. A biography about Wolfgang Mozart taken mainly from the many letters the composer; his sister, Nannerl; and his father, Leopold, wrote during their lifetimes.

Hans T. David and Arthur Mendel, eds., *The Bach Reader*. New York: W. W. Norton, 1966. First published in 1945, this book details the life and times of Johann Sebastian Bach in his own words and those of his contemporaries by using source letters and documents gathered together in one volume for the first time.

Alfred Einstein, *Mozart: His Character and His Work*. New York: Oxford University Press, 1945. This book discusses the brilliant works of Mozart and analyzes the character of the former child prodigy, who remained something of a child well into his adult life.

David Ewen, *The Complete Book of Classical Music*. Englewood Cliffs, NJ: Prentice-Hall, 1965. A weighty book filled with the life stories and musical analyses of great composers from Bach to Tchaikovsky to Strauss. The author is one of the most widely published music writers in the world.

———, *George Gershwin: His Journey to Greatness*. New York: Ungar, 1986. First published in 1970, this is the only book written since the 1930s by someone who was a personal friend of George Gershwin. Ewen has written biographies of other composers, including Jerome Kern, Leonard Bernstein, and others.

Hans Gal, ed., *The Musician's World*. New York: Arco, 1965. A book of letters written by and sent to dozens of great composers, including Bach, Mozart, and Puccini. Also included are letters from composers to other composers and letters written by famous friends and family members of composers.

Isaac Goldberg, *Gershwin: A Study in American Music.* New York: Frederick Ungar, 1958. The first biographical account of George Gershwin written in 1931, several years before the composer died. The author was one of the foremost critics of his day, lectured at Harvard University, and personally knew Gershwin.

Howard Greenfeld, *Puccini.* New York: G. P. Putnam's Sons, 1980. A biography of Puccini based largely on the extensive correspondence written and received by the composer. Many of these items are translated into English for the first time here.

Edward Jablonski, *Gershwin.* New York: G. P. Putnam's Sons, 1962. An absorbing biography of George Gershwin from an author who was a musical columnist and author of several books on the Gershwins and other composers.

Stanley Jackson, *Monsieur Butterfly.* New York: Stein and Day, 1974. A biography of Puccini that shows the great composer as a down-to-earth man who loved to play practical jokes while dazzling the world with his operatic talents.

Gerald McKnight, *Andrew Lloyd Webber.* New York: St. Martin's, 1984. The first biography written about one of the twentieth century's most popular musical composers, written with the benefit of many long interviews with Lloyd Webber and his colleagues.

Ellis Nassour and Richard Broderick, *Rock Opera.* New York: Hawthorn Books, 1973. A book the covers the creation of Andrew Lloyd Webber's rock opera *Jesus Christ Superstar,* from its inception as an idea to a Broadway musical and major motion picture.

Ates Orga, *Beethoven: His Life and Times.* Neptune City, NJ: Paganiniana, 1980. An oversized book with many black-and-white drawings, sheet music reproductions, and source quotes that illustrate the life of Ludwig van Beethoven.

Alexander Orlova, *Tchaikovsky: A Self-Portrait.* New York: Oxford University Press, 1990. This book with extensive quotes from the diaries and writings of Tchaikovsky takes the reader through the composer's emotional and difficult life. Between Tchaikovsky's writings, author Orlova moves the story along with facts and unmentioned episodes.

Joan Peyser, *The Memory of All That.* New York: Simon & Schuster, 1993. Peyser is the author of several well-known books about music and has written for the *New York Times* and the *Musical Quarterly.* Her book about Gershwin goes beyond the mere biographical and attempts to illuminate the real man behind the musical star.

Mary Jane Phillips-Matz, "Verdi's Heir," *Opera News,* March 2, 1996. An article about Giuseppe Verdi's influence on Giacomo Puccini with in-depth biographical information about the Italian composer.

Erich Schenk, *Mozart and His Times.* New York: Knopf, 1959. The author of this book was born in Salzburg in 1902 and held the chair in musicology at the University of Vienna. For thirty years, his many books and articles were hailed as major contributions to musical history and musicology.

Harold C. Schonberg, *The Lives of the Great Composers.* New York: W. W. Norton, 1981. This book details the life of great composers from the Renaissance era to modern times and is written by the senior music critic of the *New York Times,* who was awarded a Pulitzer Prize for criticism in 1971.

Charles Schwartz, *Gershwin: His Life and Music.* Indianapolis: Bobbs-Merrill, 1973. An in-depth book about George Gershwin, his life, and his times with an introduction by world-famous conductor and composer Leonard Bernstein.

Albert Schweitzer, *J. S. Bach.* Vol. 1. New York: Dover, 1966. This volume, first published in 1911, was written by famous humanitarian Albert Schweitzer, who was also a highly qualified musicologist. This book is considered one of the classic studies of the composer's life.

O. G. Sonneck, ed., *Beethoven: Impressions by His Contemporaries.* New York: Dover, 1967. This book, first published in 1926, records the words written about Ludwig van Beethoven by thirty-nine men who met the genius and lived during his era. Offers interesting source quotes from those who actually heard the master play.

Piotr Ilyich Tchaikovsky, *Letters to His Family: An Autobiography.* New York: Stein and Day, 1981. Tchaikovsky wrote many long letters to friends and relatives during his short fifty-three years—enough to fill more than 550 pages of this book with his joy, sadness, and day-to-day progress as one of the nineteenth century's most famous composers.

Charles Sanford Terry, *Johann Sebastian Bach.* London: Oxford University Press, 1972. First published in 1928, this scholarly work is a formal catalog of the composer's life rather than a critical appreciation of his music. Contains many photos and drawings of places Bach worked and lived and includes a detailed family tree.

Alexander Thayer, *The Life of Ludwig van Beethoven.* Vols. 1 and 3. Ann Arbor, MI: University Microfilms International, 1989. These books are facsimiles made from the master copy of the original book printed in 1866. Thayer, who was one of Beethoven's first biographers, wrote three volumes about the composer. Thayer began writing only twenty years after Beethoven's death, and he continued his writing until his own death thirty years later. This long, detailed biography is the central document on which many other books about Beethoven have been based.

Herbert Weinstock, *Tchaikovsky*. New York: Knopf, 1959. When first published in 1943, this book was the first biography of Pyotr Ilich Tchaikovsky ever written in English.

INDEX

PICTURE CREDITS

ABOUT THE AUTHOR

Stuart A. Kallen is the author of more than 150 nonfiction books for children and young adults. He has written on topics ranging from the theory of relativity and rock-and-roll history to life on the American frontier. In addition, Mr. Kallen has written award-winning children's videos and television scripts. In his spare time, Stuart A. Kallen is a singer/songwriter/guitarist in San Diego, California.